A Guide to
Sunday School
Enlargement

A Guide to Sunday School Enlargement

GEORGE W. STUART, Compiler

Convention Press
NASHVILLE, TENNESSEE

Foreword

THIS BOOK was written because of a deep need to help churches reach the growing multitudes of unreached, unchurched, and untaught people for Bible study and obedience to Christ. The book discusses basic Sunday School growth principles. It is our prayer that, as these principles are studied and applied, churches' concern for reaching people may be revived.

The people who need to be reached are real persons, and their spiritual needs are basic. The Holy Spirit leads in meeting these needs through the teaching and preaching of the Word of God.

The challenge of unreached persons compels every church to evaluate the progress that has been made in involving more persons in Bible study and to determine the directions that must be taken to meet new times and new demands.

The world has moved swiftly into the space age with its vast possibilities and unknown needs. Churches today want to be prepared to serve in this age. This is a time for reappraisal of objectives and goals. In a period of change, new methods are needed. However, certain basic spiritual factors remain the same:

- God's concern for the individual
- Jesus Christ's love for all mankind
- The gospel—simple yet powerful
- The spiritual needs of persons
- Christ's commission to his church
- Principles of Sunday School growth that work

If this book achieves its purpose, it will help churches focus on the individuals in their midst: the man, the woman; the young person, the child; all persons. These persons need to be cultivated through visitation. They need to be involved in Bible study so that they will be confronted with God's provision for salvation through Jesus Christ. This book can help Sunday School leaders and members see the need to increase their efforts to involve people in Bible study. This enlargement study will focus on the Bible teaching program as the church expressing itself in outreach for the unreached.

A church must look at the expanding population, think clearly and objectively about its responsibility, and take the necessary actions to reach these persons. No matter what adjustments in organization and space may be necessary, no matter what new approaches may need to be taken, the goals of the Lord Jesus point the way: "Go ye therefore, and teach all nations, baptizing them in the name of the Father, and of the Son, and of the Holy Ghost: teaching them to observe all things whatsoever I have commanded you: and, lo, I am with you alway, even unto the end of the world" (Matt. 28 : 19–20).

A writing team has prepared this book, working from outlines prepared jointly by the team. The team consisted of Howard P. Colson, Earl Waldrup, John T. Sisemore, Daryl Heath, Harold C. Marsh, Rowland E. Crowder, Chester Vaughn, and James W. Chatham.

GEORGE W. STUART

(Editor's Note: Mr. Stuart was a consultant in the Sunday School Department, Sunday School Board, until his death in January, 1972.)

Contents

1

THE BIBLICAL BASIS
for Enlargement[1]

SOME PERSONS seem to regard a Bible teaching enlargement program with a degree of skepticism. They apparently think of it merely as a scheme to increase the number of names on a Sunday School roll. Actually, an enlargement program is more significant than this. The motive behind it is much deeper than just a desire to pile up statistics.

A Sunday School enlargement program includes all the efforts that a church, through its Sunday School, makes to discover the persons for whom it is responsible, to provide thoughtful Bible study opportunities for them, and to enlist these persons in such study and response to Bible truth.

This kind of program is intended to open the way for the church's ministry and witness and to bring as many persons as possible into an increasingly meaningful relationship with Christ and the church.

Whenever any phase of Christian responsibility is under consideration, it is right to raise the question, What is the teaching of the Bible about this matter? In line with that viewpoint, this chapter is concerned with the biblical basis for Sunday School enlargement.

We cannot find in the Bible an actual description of the process of enlargement in terms of present-day organization. But we do have the right, and the responsibility, to look into the Word of God in search of principles by which to guide our ideas, objectives, and methods for outreach. Such principles should help us in formulating practical plans for reaching more persons for Bible study. Only in the measure in which our enlargement efforts rest on scriptural foundations, are geared to scriptural objectives, and are carried out in the spirit of Christ, can we expect them to have divine approval and blessing.

Before we are ready to think about means and methods, we must ask: How is our effort to reach more people for Bible study related to such matters as God's purposes for man, the nature and needs of man, and the nature and mission of a church?

I. The Purposes of God for Man

In Genesis 1:26–28, we are told that God made man in his image and gave him dominion over everything on the earth. Let us consider two great divine purposes which may be discerned in this basic, ancient statement: *fellowship* and *dominion.*

1. Fellowship

The highest privilege possible to a human being is to know, love, trust, and obey God. The fact that man was created in God's own image means that man has the capacity for fellowship with God. Only a being who is free, rational, and made in the moral and spiritual image of God could ever experience the holy privileges of fellowship with God. The entire biblical revelation deals with this matter of man's fellowship with God.

In the Genesis 3 account, we see that by sin and rebellion man put himself out of fellowship with his Maker. Yet God in love has provided redemption through Jesus Christ, thus opening the way for man to return to divine fellowship. The Bible makes clear that through Christ man can enter into eternal fellowship with God; it also reveals the fact that God most deeply desires man to do so. Herein lies the basis of redemption, the church, evangelism, outreach, and missions.

Implied in the possibility of man's fellowship with God is the possibility of a fellowship between man and man transcending every other human relationship. For as men are redeemed by Christ and become children of God, they thereby become brothers or sisters of all God's other children. Thus the church is the family of God. And it is God's will that every one of his redeemed children enjoy to the full the fellowship of a warmhearted, brotherly, compassionate, soul-strengthening, local church. To this end, a church must pursue a program of outreach toward unenlisted Christians.

2. Dominion over the Earth

From the beginning, God gave man dominion over all the earth. Of one thing we may be certain: God intended for man to dominate the earth in such a manner as to promote the good of all mankind. In many ways a person can be a blessing to others, but in no other way can he so bless his fellowman as when he shares with him the knowledge of redemption which is in Christ Jesus. Such sharing calls for an outreach ministry on the part of a church.

II. The Nature and Needs of Man

A realization of what man is and what he can become will constrain a church to enlarge its outreach.

1. Man's Capacity for Good and Evil

Man, as created by God, has the capacity for both good and evil, and God has endowed him with the power of free choice. But through a selfish desire to have his own way, man rebels against God's righteous requirements. The only way his sinful inclination can be changed is by the miracle of regeneration. As Jesus told Nicodemus, every man must be born anew, that is, born from above, from God (John 3:3). In regeneration man's capacity for good comes to its highest potential. Although the unregenerate person can do many good things, only man redeemed can become what God intends for him to be. How can he be redeemed unless he hears the gospel? How will he hear if no church seeks him out?

2. Man's Need for Reconciliation

The root problem which the Christian gospel solves is man's estrangement from God. The story of Adam and Eve's fall into sin accurately represents the experience of every human being except Jesus. "All have sinned, and come short of the glory of God" (Rom. 3:23). In sin man insists on having his own way. He disobeys God, goes contrary to the will of God, substitutes self for God. Man's rebellion is deliberate and voluntary. We must never overlook the fact that Adam and Eve, though enticed by the tempter, were not coerced into breaking God's law. They disobeyed because they chose to do so. They refused God's rightful rule over their lives. Such rebellion is the universal nature of sin.

In describing sin, the Bible uses such words as transgression, lawlessness, ungodliness, lust, and unrighteousness. These ugly words picture man's sin as breaking bounds and going into forbidden territory, as transgressing God's law, as refusing to acknowledge God (Rom. 1:28), as setting one's desires on that which is forbidden (Eph. 2:3), and as standing for all that is contrary to God.

The sinner is in the position of being hostile both to God and to his own best interests. The Bible characterizes him as estranged, lost, dead and condemned (Gen. 3:8–10; Eph. 2:1; John 3:18). What does the sinner need to do in order to be condemned? Exactly nothing; he is condemned already. And without purposeful, loving outreach on the part of some Christian or group of Christians, that is exactly what great multitudes of sinners will do. They will do nothing about accepting Christ and his way of salvation, and so they will be eternally lost. They will be separated from God.

Man needs to be reconciled to God. Apart from Christ he is hopeless. "There is none other name under heaven given among men, whereby we must be saved" (Acts 4:12). The appeal of the gospel is, "Be ye reconciled to God" (2 Cor. 5:20).

Here, then, is a basic reason churches must be concerned about reaching more people with the gospel message. Man is a sinner standing in need of redemption. The gospel is not good advice. It is good news. It promises life abundant and eternal to those who will receive it on the divine conditions. To reach out to others with good advice may be commendable, but to reach out with the good news of God's redeeming grace is imperative. The persons to be reached with the gospel are not people going to heaven anyway, who simply need the social benefits of a religious organization. They are persons in a predicament so serious that only the saving grace of God can deliver them from it.

Man's need for reconciliation to God provides strong motivation for churches to make a loving outreach to the lost. In the last analysis, an enlarged Bible teaching program is an effort to enrol persons in Bible study. The desired result of such a program is to lead the lost persons to become reconciled to God.

3. Man's Need for Meaningful Involvement in a Church

No sinner can be saved by a church; he can only be saved by Christ. But, under ordinary conditions, God's plan for reaching the sinner is for a church, as a loving fellowship of redeemed persons, to reach out and surround the sinner with the warmth of Christian love in such a way that he will come to realize his need, discover the provision God has made for meeting it, and then commit himself to Christ as Lord and Savior. One of the most effective ways of bringing persons to Christ is to involve them in Bible study. Reaching lost persons and teaching them the gospel message are major tasks of the church if the lost are to be reconciled to God. But Christians must have loving concern for persons who need a redemptive witness.

Furthermore, the lives of many professing Christians manifest a disturbing lack of spiritual growth. Such persons are missing the riches God has for them. Unconfessed and unforgiven sin in their lives results in loss of fellowship with Christ. They are defeated because they are grieving the indwelling Spirit of God. A church's enlargement efforts must include persons who are church members but who seem unconcerned about being a part of the church's life. Outreach for such persons is a response to the instructions of the New Testament: "We . . . that are strong ought to bear the infirmities of the weak" (Rom. 15:1). "Brethren, if a man be overtaken in a fault, ye which are spiritual, restore such an one" (Gal. 6:1). "Let us consider one another to provoke [stir up] unto love and to good works" (Heb. 10:24).

Another group of persons to be reached for Bible study in a Sunday School's enlargement plans is the children. The younger ones are not yet accountable, but we have the strongest of reasons for seeking to enrol them in the church's Bible teaching program. If they are thus involved, the probability of their coming to a saving knowledge of Christ is far greater than it is if they are spiritually neglected in their early years. Experience has abundantly proved this point.

III. The Nature and Mission of a Church

Understanding the nature and mission of a church is of the highest importance. Failure to do so will inevitably lead to wrong attitudes toward the church and the neglect of its claims and mission. The nature and mission of a church demand that, if it is to "be a church," it must reach out and confront individuals and social groups with a message concerning God's plan.

1. *The Nature of a Church*

The New Testament presents the nature of a church in a variety of ways. Among other things, a church is a covenant fellowship of love, a colony of heaven on earth, and the body of Christ.

(1) *A covenant fellowship of love.*—Ancient Israel was God's covenant people. He chose them to be his own in a unique sense. To this people he gave a special revelation of his nature and his will. But he did not choose them for their own sake. He chose them that they might be a blessing to the world, a missionary na-

tion to bring to other peoples a knowledge of the true and living God. In a real and profound sense, Israel *was* a missionary people. For instance, by God's grace, the Old Testament was their gift to the world. And Jesus, in his human background, was a Jew. But in a tragic way, Israel as a nation failed to perform her missionary function. She came to be more concerned about her own internal affairs than about reaching out in love to bring the knowledge of the Lord to the rest of the world.

The New Testament church is God's covenant people today. The old covenant with Israel was sealed with the blood of sacrificial animals; the new covenant with the church has been sealed with the blood of Christ. Furthermore, stronger ties bind New Testament Christians together in love than the ties which bound the people of ancient Israel. True, they were all of one race and had experienced many mighty acts of God for their deliverance. But the New Testament church is bound together in a far greater way—in a common experience of the redeeming love of Christ. Nothing can produce a truer fellowship than this. Our fellowship includes not only our love for Christ and love for one another; it also includes love for all of those for whom Christ died. As Paul so aptly wrote, "We are ruled by Christ's love for us, now that we recognize that one man died for all men, which means that all men take part in his death. He died for all men so that those who live should no longer live for themselves, but only for him who died and was raised to life for their sake" (2 Cor. 5:14–15, TEV).[2]

(2) *A colony of heaven on earth.*—The New Testament pictures a church as a colony of heaven. According to the King James Version, Paul said that "our conversation is in heaven" (Phil. 3:20). But the Greek word translated "conversation" really means "citizenship." Today's English Version translates it, "We . . . are citizens of heaven." Paul was referring to the fact that the city of Philippi had the status of a colony of Rome, the imperial capital. Not only was such a colony governed by the same statutes as the mother city; it was a veritable miniature of that city. Its citizens enjoyed the same privileges and immunities as did those living on the very banks of the Tiber. They took great pride in their citizenship and

sought to honor Rome by the way they conducted their affairs.

When Paul told the church at Philippi that they were a colony of heaven, they knew what he meant. They knew that they were a highly privileged people, whose capital city was heaven itself. They also knew that as representatives of heaven they were to live their lives on earth in accordance with heavenly principles (see Matt. 6:10). They were to live for the honor and glory of their Lord.

The concept of a church as a colony of heaven has much to teach us about what a church should be and do (see Eph. 2:19; Col. 3:1). Since a prime concern of heaven is the winning of men to Christ, a prime concern of a church should be the same. The bearing of this fact upon church outreach and Sunday School enlargement should be obvious.

(3) *The body of Christ.*—The phrase "the body of Christ" probably is the most significant of all the New Testament descriptions of the church. (See Rom. 12:4-5; 1 Cor. 12:12-27; Eph. 1:22-23; 2:16; 3:6; 4:4,12; Col. 1:18,24.) The description is very suggestive. It speaks of a living union between Christ and his people. Furthermore, it implies oneness of purpose. It points to the fact that a church is the agent, instrument, or vehicle by which Christ accomplishes his purposes. It suggests the readiness with which the church, as the body of Christ, should carry out the expressed will of its divine Head.

2. The Mission of a Church

Toward unredeemed men, the church is to be the agent of reconciliation—the liaison between Christ and the lost. For the reconciled it is to be a redemptive family, furnishing wholesome environment and nurture for spiritual growth.

(1) *The agent of reconciliation.*—Since Christ came to seek and to save the lost, the mission of a church becomes clear. He has commanded us to make disciples, to be his witnesses. If we refuse or neglect to make a constant loving effort to reach people in his name, we as members of his body are being disloyal to our Head. When a church, through its Bible teaching program, makes plans

for reaching more persons for Bible study, it must not be accused of making a mere bid for numbers. What it is really doing, if it conceives of the effort aright, is helping carry out Christ's purpose to win as many persons as possible for his kingdom. What could be truer to Christ and the New Testament than this?

(2) *The redemptive family of the reconciled.*—Not only is a church to serve as an agent of reconciliation, it also is to function as the redemptive family of the reconciled. When lost persons are reconciled to God, it is not his will that they should live out their new life in isolated detachment from other Christians. All Christians, as children of God, are brothers of one another. In this sense, therefore, a church is a family. Just as the divine plan is for new-born babies to belong to parents and be nurtured in the atmosphere of loving family relations, God wills that his reconciled spiritual children should live and grow in the loving atmosphere of a church. Conceivably someone might be a saved individual and yet not be living in fellowship with a church, but such a separated life is most unnatural and undesirable.

In present-day American life many individuals and families move their places of residence frequently. Many persons who have had a relationship to a church in a previous location fail, for one reason or another, to relate to a church in their new location. The large number of nonresident church members is one of the greatest problems in church work today. The tragedy of this problem is at least twofold.

Most of these nonresident members are losing out spiritually for lack of what a local church could do for them. On the other hand, the local church is missing out on what these potential members could do for it. For these reasons, an important aspect of Sunday School enlargement is the bringing of nonresident members into the fellowship of the church. Enrolling such people for Bible study is a first step toward getting them meaningfully involved in the total life of a church.

We have now seen that the biblical basis for enlargement includes God's purposes for man, the nature and needs of man, and the nature and mission of a church. One more aspect of the subject remains to be considered—the priesthood of all believers. This great reality of the Christian faith has a relationship to the matter of enlargement which many Christians may never have recognized or thought about.

IV. The Priesthood of All Believers

In ancient Israel only a select group of men were privileged to serve as priests—that is, to represent God to the people and to represent the people before God. But under the new covenant in Christ, all of God's people are priests. God has chosen them "to be a holy priesthood, to offer spiritual sacrifices acceptable to God through Jesus Christ" and to "declare the wonderful deeds of him who called you [them] out of darkness into his marvelous light" (1 Peter 2:5,9, RSV).

One highly significant aspect of Christian priesthood is this: God desires to make a loving outreach to those who are as yet strangers to his grace. Each Christian fulfils a part of his calling as a priest when he brings the Word of God to men and brings men to Christ. What can be more satisfying to a Christian than thus to fulfil his divine calling?

The outreach efforts of a local church through its Sunday School may become a part of God's redemptive plan of the ages. What significance this fact gives to Sunday School enlargement, which might otherwise be "just another scheme" to increase statistics!

1. *The Example to Be Followed*

In the chapter in which Peter referred to the church as a holy priesthood, we find a verse which clearly points out the example a church—and that means its members—should follow in serving God. Peter was dealing with the fact that his readers could expect to endure suffering for Christ's sake. In this connection he wrote: "For even hereunto were ye called: because Christ also suffered for us, leaving us an example, that ye should follow his steps" (1 Peter 2:21).

In following the steps of Jesus today, we may or may not have to endure persecution as many of the early Christians did. But we cannot follow his steps and fail to go out to reach persons for God. Think of how many loving steps Jesus took while on earth in his passion to bring men to God! In this he is our example. Going out after prospects is not a part of some clever, man-made scheme. It is following the steps of Jesus in seeking the lost and the straying. Is he not saying to us today what he said to his disciples of old, "As my Father hath sent me, even so send I you" (John 20:21)?

2. A Demonstration of Faith Versus a Profession of Faith

The New Testament is unmistakably clear in its emphasis on the necessity of genuine faith in Christ. But it is equally clear in its demand that those who profess faith demonstrate their faith in life. If we profess to believe in Jesus, we must prove our faith by our actions. This principle holds for both individuals and churches. If a church professes to believe in and follow Christ, it has the inescapable obligation of reaching out in his name to win others to him. Being satisfied with results already attained is not enough. We must reach more persons for him, otherwise our profession of faith is an impertinence. One of the ways we demonstrate our faith and our commitment is by serious and sustained efforts to bring into his fold as many as possible of the people for whose sake he died and arose.

3. Salvation by Grace, Through Faith, to Works

In one of the great passages in which Paul dealt with the subject of salvation, he emphasized the principle with which we are here concerned: Salvation is *by* grace *through* faith, *to* works. In Ephesians 2:8–10 the relationship between what God has done for us and what we should be doing for him is clearly set forth. Verses 8 and 9 make a great, basic declaration: "By grace are ye saved through faith; and that not of yourselves: it is the gift of God: not of works, lest any man should boast." All evangelical Christians rejoice in the truth there stated, that our salvation is by grace through faith. But we must never be satisfied to stop at that point. In verse 10 we see the intention God had in saving us:

"We are his workmanship, created in Christ Jesus unto good works." We are saved for good works. That is, God intends for us to do his work in the world. And an important part of that work is reaching persons for Christ's eternal kingdom.

4. The Covenant Commitments of Church Membership

If a person is truly a child of God, born of his Spirit, and a member of the body of Christ, the very profession of faith which he made, before he was baptized and received into the local fellowship, implies that he has yielded himself to the will of his divine Lord and Savior. As we have seen, high on the priorities of the Savior's program is the Commission to make disciples and to teach them to do his will (Matt. 28 : 19–20). The point here is that every church member is involved. His involvement is inherent in his church membership. Therefore, we can affirm in all fairness that every member of a Baptist church has at least some obligation in the direction of helping his church to bring others under the influence of the teaching of God's Word.

In summary, we may say that the purposes of a rightly conceived Sunday School enlargement program rest on a sound, scriptural basis. Since God created man with a view to his living in eternal fellowship with his Creator, and since God, in his infinite love and grace, has in Christ provided eternal salvation for man the sinner, all who know the Savior are compelled to make known the way of salvation to persons who do not know it. Apart from Christ there is no salvation. The church is the divinely appointed agent of reconciliation between a loving God and sinful men. As a covenant fellowship of love, as a colony of heaven, and as the body of Christ on earth, a church has the holy task of reaching out for people who without its loving concern might never come to know the Savior's love.

All believers have a part in the program of Christian outreach. They must follow the example of their Lord. They must demonstrate their faith by their actions. They must realize that they have been saved for service, and that the covenant commitments of their church membership call upon them to aid in making disciples and in teaching these disciples to do the Master's will.

Such a task, with all of its awesome responsibilities, calls upon a church to find the best ways of accomplishing the work. One of the soundest approaches toward helping persons come to know the Lord in personal, saving experience is that of involving them in meaningful Bible study. Therefore, the more persons who can be enlisted for Bible study, the greater the likelihood that many will be brought to a saving knowledge of Christ, will find their places in the fellowship of the redeemed, will join in Christian service, and will grow toward Christian maturity.

The kind of Sunday School enlargement program described in the succeeding chapters of this book is geared to this thoroughly biblical and Christian purpose. Let no one say that such a program is a mere man-made scheme. Surely God is in it when its purpose is so fully in keeping with the divine intent.

---

[1] Parts of this chapter reproduce sections or ideas found in the first chapter of the study course book, *Reaching All Prospects for the Church* (Nashville: Convention Press, 1964), pp. 1–14.

[2] *Good News for Modern Man: The New Testament in Today's English Version* (© American Bible Society, New York, 1966). This and all other quotations are used by permission.

2

THE NEEDS AND GOALS
for Enlargement

WE HAVE SEEN in chapter 1 that at least three factors stand out as biblical guidelines to a church's efforts to reach and involve persons in its life and witness: (1) The nature and needs of persons are such that they are incomplete without a vital relationship to Christ and his church. (2) The nature and mission of a church demand a vital and relevant church outreach to the lost. (3) The priesthood of all believers requires that all church members have a significant role in the outreach ministry of their church. These are basic considerations to an understanding of enlargement.

I. Do We Need to Enlarge Our Sunday Schools?

Should *every* Sunday School grow? This question is pondered by many thoughtful churchmen when a Sunday School enlargement emphasis is considered. Does every church really need to enlarge its Sunday School? Obviously, before this question can be answered, some other questions need to be asked and answered. If by enlargement we mean simply adding more units and more leaders to the existing organization, some churches do not need

14

to enlarge. Though this type of enlargement is one of the major emphases of this book, considerably more is envisioned for most churches. Meeting enlargement needs involves many related benefits.

1. Organizational Balance

Caring for enlargement needs involves frequent adjustment of the organization to relate to present enrolment and prospect needs. Sudden population shifts and other social and economic changes often necessitate organizational changes in a church. Some churches have too few units in some age groups, while they may be able to do effective work with fewer units in other age groups.

2. Work Improvement

A concerted program of enlargement produces general improvement of its Bible teaching program. When officers and teachers engage in serious study of their organizational needs—including size, function, and purpose of each unit—improvement is almost inevitable. There may be situations in which the census, possibilities study, and review of the present organization suggest little or no organizational enlargement. However, most Sunday School officers and teachers who make such a study will approach work through their present organization with greater enthusiasm and dedication. Furthermore, their efficiency is greatly improved through the clarification of responsibilities and methods by which responsibilities are carried out.

3. New Sunday Schools

Basic to Southern Baptist Sunday School growth in the past has been the practice of forming new classes and departments. That new units grow faster, win more people to Christ, and provide more workers to carry on the work of the church is a recognized fact. Following this principle, large departments and classes sometimes are divided to form new units. The results usually are enrolment and attendance increases with the other fruits which are produced by increased involvement in Bible study.

However, many churches have reached the point that they need to take seriously another facet of this principle. New units may be formed within the church, or they may be formed beyond the church in a new location. Such a unit may be what is sometimes called a fellowship Bible class. A fellowship Bible class is a Bible study group, usually meeting in an apartment or a home, for the purpose of Bible study, prayer, fellowship, and Christian witnessing. The home may be in a community needing a new Sunday School through which a new church can be established eventually. Many Southern Baptist churches have not understood and applied this facet of the principle of growth through new units. Sometimes new units beyond the church not only are not planned, but are viewed as a threat to the church's prosperity.

No one can say when a church is big enough. However, most thoughtful churchmen do agree that when a church is large enough to carry on a full program, the time has come to adopt a systematic plan for regularly channeling some of its resources into the formation of new churches. This may be done in its own community or in a community where outside assistance is needed. One of the greatest fruits of a Sunday School enlargement campaign may be the decision of a church to establish a new unit of work beyond the walls of its own building.

4. Organizational Enlargement

Considering the question, Does every church need to enlarge its Sunday School? let us try to formulate an answer.

When enlargement is viewed in its broadest sense, every church does need to enlarge its Bible teaching program. Vision needs to be lifted; assignments need to be clarified; methodology needs to be sharpened; and the church generally needs to recommit itself to the goals normally pursued through the Sunday School. When enlargement is viewed in the more limited organizational sense, not every church needs to enlarge its Sunday School organization. However, churches will benefit from a periodic review of their organization, and many of them need to give serious consideration to the formation of new units of work in areas where people are not being reached by some other church.

II. Man's Primary Need

In our day of material affluence and intellectual sophistication, it is easy to lose sight of man's primary need: namely, his need for a transforming encounter with Christ and a continuing experience of growth and service in his name. A millionaire without Christ is just as lost and condemned before God as a pauper who does not know Christ. A person's economic and intellectual attainments do not alter his need for the redemptive work of Christ. A person's place and influence in the important places of leadership in the community do not change his need for Christ. All men—rich and poor, learned and unlearned—stand before God with the same basic need.

Bible study provides the best platform on which lost men can be brought to a meaningful encounter with God through Christ. Churches which are making significant efforts in the area of church renewal are concluding that a meaningful and well-supported plan of Bible study is the foundation of all other work which a church is called upon to do. Thus, when a church takes a look at its Bible teaching program, it is focusing on a foundational ministry and one which provides the means for addressing man's most basic need.

III. Three Foundational Tasks

When planning for the enlargement of the Sunday School, it is important to keep in mind the total content and scope of the program. Most churches seek to perform three major tasks through their Sunday Schools: (1) Teach the biblical revelation (usually referred to simply as "Bible teaching"). (2) Reach persons for Christ and church membership (often referred to as "outreach"). (3) Perform the functions of the church within its constituency (lead all church members to worship, learn, witness, minister, and apply Bible truth). Bible teaching becomes a goal for the church's outreach to the lost and unenlisted and is a primary means toward meaningful involvement of Christians in the church's life and witness. Sunday School enlargement is concerned with enlarging the church's efforts in these three areas of the Christian life.

1. Outreach

The outreach task has both an external and an internal focus. It points the church to the multitudes of lost people who have no church connection and defines the church's evangelistic responsibility. It also points the church to the lost who are involved in Sunday School and the thousands who have their names on the church roll but give little or no evidence of knowing the church's Lord. There is increasing evidence that one of the needs of modern churches is a warm, loving evangelistic witness to many church members who, by any biblical criteria, are church members in name only. They have not been born again and, therefore, cannot be members of Christ's body. Reaching out in love and sincerity to such persons is an important means by which a church should seek to be a regenerate fellowship capable of understanding and responding to the commission of its Lord.

2. Bible Teaching

The Bible teaching task likewise has a dual focus. It provides the preparation which the lost person needs in order to hear and respond to the call of Christ to salvation. It also provides the principal diet for growing Christians as they attempt to function as servants and priests, both in the church and in the world (1 Peter 2:9). Study of the biblical revelation points the church to the broader and continuing dimensions of discipleship, emphasizing that church members need to "observe all things" that Christ commanded (Matt. 28:20).

The way of the "broad road, the wide gate, and easy discipleship," which characterizes many churches today, is being tried and found wanting. "Cheap grace" is too costly to be tolerated by a church when the world is in revolution. Christ's invitation was, and still is: "'If any man would come after me, let him deny himself and take up his cross and follow me. For whoever would save his life will lose it, and whoever loses his life for my sake will find it'" (Matt. 16 : 24–25, RSV). This is costly grace. The demands of discipleship are death to self and the crowning of Christ as the Lord of life. In no other practical way can a church continually call lost people and its own members to this kind of discipleship except in the context and climate of serious Bible study.

3. Christian Living

The task of leading church members to worship, learn, witness, minister, and apply Bible truth is the outgrowth of the continuing outreach and Bible teaching tasks. It seeks to involve church members in performing the functions of a church, sending them back into the outreach and teaching arenas. Like the other two tasks, this task has a dual focus—internal and external. It focuses on the functioning of the members in the corporate life of the church in such a way that the church continues to be the church Christ intended it to be. It focuses on the performance of Christians in the world beyond the church building. Leading all church members to perform the functions of a church involves keeping the members aware that being a Christian is a seven-day-a-week calling. Christian involvement does not end as Bible study and the worship service closes on Sunday. In a real sense, it only begins then, as Christians go out to penetrate with love the life of the world that surrounds them.

4. Outreach, Bible Teaching, Performance

For practical implementation each of the three tasks—reaching, teaching, performing—is viewed separately. Yet they must be viewed together if their full significance is to be realized. They are different tasks in that they represent distinct areas of human and church need. Yet they are inseparable tasks in that one cannot be accomplished without doing the others.

These three tasks relate to basic goals that are essential to the nature and mission of a church: (1) to be a regenerate fellowship that bears and responds to a valid Christian witness; (2) to be a disciplined, learning fellowship that lives and works under the lordship of Christ; and (3) to be a warm, loving fellowship which, by example and teaching, leads its members to meaningful involvement in the functions of a New Testament church. This is what following Christ faithfully is all about.

Outreach, Bible teaching, and performance are, in a sense, only facets of a larger goal which is inherent in Christ's commission to his church. They can be divided and assigned to individuals for implementation, but they must be viewed as a whole if any part of the goal is to be genuinely accomplished. Outreach that leaves people at the baptismal pool is not biblical evangelism. Bible teaching that leaves class members content to enjoy the comforts and fellowship of the classroom without going out to seek others is shallow and hypocritical. Performance that does not involve both a vital corporate church life and a witness with integrity in the world falls short of the New Testament ideal.

Thus Sunday School enlargement, though specific in focus and geared at times to the immediate organizational needs of a church, looks beyond these needs to goals which are so broad and comprehensive that they touch the entire nature and mission of the church.

IV. Related Church Actions Toward Mature Discipleship

Consider further the three tasks already discussed: reaching all prospects for Christ and church membership; teaching the biblical revelation; and performing the functions of the church within its constituency. These tasks relate to all that a church is and seeks to do. Yet their accomplishment requires that other actions be taken by the church. Normally these other actions are performed through other organizations of the church. Four of these are very important to a vital Bible teaching program.

1. Giving Orientation to New Church Members

This ministry is normally implemented through the church training program. But it is essential to the success of church actions which are taken through the Sunday School. New church member orientation is a plan for involving new members in the fellowship which they have joined. It is a church's planned approach to assuring a valid church relationship for converted persons. From this valid relationship, new members can be guided and encouraged toward effective Christian discipleship. Furthermore, although orientation is a continuing program of a church, it is a short-term experience for the new member. His new relationship to Christ in the church is interpreted to him. He is helped to become seriously involved in the life of his church and its witness to the world as an ongoing commitment of himself to Christ.

In new church member orientation, a church is concerned with at least two things: a specific ministry to all persons who seek church membership, and the integrity of its own example and witness. The following makes a worthy objective: *to minister wisely to all new members while preserving the purity and strength of the church for kingdom service.*

This statement of objective contains two basic concepts. The first concerns a wise ministry to all persons who present themselves for church membership. The second involves the integrity of witness and the strength of a church. The order in which the two concepts are stated is of importance.

A church's basic mission is to win persons to Christ and bring them into the fellowship of his church. Here they can worship, grow, and serve. The Bible makes clear that only converted persons are to be baptized and become members of the body of Christ. A saving experience with Jesus Christ so transforms a person's life that he desires to affiliate with others of like experience. A church must assume the responsibility to let itself be used by the Holy Spirit to perform the delicate and often time-consuming work of leading persons to this saving experience, which is the basic qualification for church membership.

The biblical doctrine of a regenerate church membership includes another idea. It emphasizes the importance of maintaining the purity and increasing the strength of the corporate body of believers. A church must be vigilant to express in practice and witness the scriptural meaning of church membership. This is necessary if the Holy Spirit is to work freely and effectively in and through the church.

The purpose of new church member orientation, which is usually provided by the church training program, may be restated as three separate objectives:

(1) To help each new member and the church to be assured that the new member is converted to Christ and that he is committed to the church

(2) To help each new member gain an adequate understanding and acceptance of the privileges and responsibilities of membership in the church

(3) To help each new member become a growing participant in the Christian fellowship, relate to the world from a Christian perspective, and bear an effective Christian witness.

2. Teaching Other Content Areas

There are several vital content areas which are closely related to the biblical revelation. For purposes of program implementation, they are separated and assigned to specific church organizations. Yet, they cannot be dealt with adequately except in the context of a total church teaching curriculum. Thus, teaching the biblical revelation, though normally implemented through the Sunday School, must be viewed in relation to other content areas which are implemented in most churches through other educational organizations.

The point is this: When thinking of Sunday School enlargement, the goals must be much broader and deeper than the immediate program goals of a particular organization. There are at least two essentials for a meaningful and valid study of the needs and methods of Sunday School enlargement. (1) The church actions normally carried out through the Bible teaching program must be viewed in relation to church actions which are carried out through other programs. (2) The total study and service needs of individuals must be recognized and planned for in both general and specific organization program planning. There is no justification for five program organizations in a church except as the five can function as one, each addressing itself to the basic needs of individuals.

3. *Training for Christian Performance*

As already pointed out, a study of current statements of church tasks reveals that many of the tasks are closely related. In no case is this relationship more true than in performing the functions of the church which include: leading church members to worship, witness, learn, minister, and apply; and training church members to do those things. Which does the church do first? This question is like asking, When shaking hands with a person, which side of the hand does one shake first? One side cannot be shaken without shaking the other, though one side of the hand is touched first. So it is with these two church tasks. Church members cannot be led to perform well unless they are trained to perform; they cannot be trained to perform unless they are led to perform. Tragic short-sightedness is evident when church leaders get so involved in a single organization that they do not see their particular program as a part of the total church mission and work to shape and direct their personal efforts to the total needs of individuals.

4. *Leadership Training—Potential and Specialized*

Sunday School enlargement, both in terms of organizational enlargement and work improvement, depends in a large measure on leadership. Both the number of leaders available and the level at which they can perform set limits beyond which a church cannot progress. Again, a church's Bible teaching program and its church training program must be viewed together. One cannot function successfully apart from the other. An adequate training program may make Sunday School leaders conscious of the need for enlargement. On the other hand, Sunday School enlargement may emphasize the need for a training program. In either case, training—both general and specialized—is vitally related to all that a church seeks to do through its Sunday School.

V. Needs and Goals Summarized

The goals that are sought in Sunday School enlargement may be stated as follows: (1) to reach people for Bible study; (2) to teach them the gospel which "is the power of God for salvation" (Rom. 1:16, RSV); (3) to win them to Christian discipleship and to church membership; (4) to develop them as Christian disciples and church members through involving them in worshiping, learning, witnessing, ministering, and applying Bible truth in daily living. Thus they become a functioning part of the effort of the church to make Christ known, loved, and obeyed by all men everywhere.

These should be the goals of every church. Some churches need to enlarge their Sunday School organization to achieve these goals. Other churches need to adjust and improve the Sunday School organization that they now have. Other churches need to establish new units in neighboring and/or distant communities where no organized Bible study opportunity is available. All churches probably need to make methods, leadership, and curriculum improvements. The following chapters are prepared with the prayer that the plans and concepts which are outlined may help churches to achieve these goals.

3

UNDERSTANDING AND APPLYING THE PRINCIPLES
of Enlargement

CHURCHES by the thousands are standing "in the midst of the multitudes." Yet 140 million persons in the United States are not under the ministry of the Bible teaching program of any church of any denomination.

Is there any way to account for this situation? Is it possible that churches have become so busy inside that they have forgotten their responsibility to take Bible study to persons on the "outside"? Do churches really take seriously their obligation to the unreached?

The members of the first church "went every where preaching the word" (Acts 8:4). Other New Testament churches followed the same pattern. As a result, in less than a century, there were Christians all over the Mediterranean world. By the end of the imperial persecutions in A.D. 313, there were multitudes of believers throughout the Roman Empire.

How did the early Christians achieve such remarkable success? The Bible gives the answer: "Daily in the temple, and in every house, they ceased not to teach and preach Jesus Christ" (Acts

5 : 42). In modern terminology, these early Christians took seriously the task of outreach.

Today Southern Baptist churches seek to reach their outsiders primarily through the Sunday School. Is it possible for a Sunday School to fulfil such an all-encompassing task? Can a modern-day Sunday School go "every where preaching the word"? Are there some basic principles, some laws of growth, which will show a church how to reap a spiritual harvest in the lives of the unreached?

To all of these questions the answer is a resounding yes. God in his wisdom has led many churches to discover some basic principles and administrative actions which have a direct bearing on Sunday School growth and, therefore, on outreach for a church. To the undiscerning eye, these principles may seem mere mechanics. But to persons with spiritual insight and vision, they become the blueprint by which Sunday Schools can accomplish their task in a way that honors Christ.

I. Principles of Enlargement Stated

Most churches are surrounded by persons who are not enrolled in Bible study. Many of these persons are not members of a church. Churches that have had a net gain in recent years have gained only three to five new persons per school. Some churches have actually lost in Sunday School enrolment. It is not surprising that the growth in church membership has been correspondingly small.

1. The Principle of Leadership

(1) *The principle stated.*—**Reaching prospects depends upon an adequate ratio of workers to enrolment and upon the degree of commitment these workers show toward their tasks.**

How can the churches come to grips with their enlistment task? The solution is not in loading more responsibility on the present Sunday School workers. The wiser course would be to put more persons to work in the outreach task. Sustained growth will not come in any other manner.

(2) *The principle interpreted.*—A study of the number of workers and of the Sunday School enrolment in the churches across

the Southern Baptist Convention has revealed a definite relationship between workers and enrolment. In almost every case, the maximum ratio for the school as a whole was a church-elected Sunday School worker for every ten members enrolled.

The proportion of members to workers will vary with each age group. The maximum recommended is as follows:

Division	Departments and/or Classes	Recommended Worker-Member Ratio	Ratio in This Church
Cradle Roll		1-6	
Preschool	B– 1	1–4	
	2– 3	1–4	
	4– 5	1–5	
Children's	6– 8 (Grades 1–3)	1–7	
	9–11 (Grades 4–6)	1–7	
Youth	12–14 (Grades 7–9)	1–10*	
	15–17 (Grades 10–12)	1–15*	
Adult	18–up	1–25*	

*Teacher-pupil ratio only

Several basic steps are necessary in attaining a good worker-member ratio.

- *Discover the present ratio.*—This is done by dividing the enrolment by the number of workers in each group. Enter this information in the column "Ratio in This Church."
- *Determine where the ratio needs to be improved.*—Keep in mind that the class or department that already has reached the maximum ratio of members to workers will reach few, if any, additional persons. Any additions that come will usually be replacements only.
- *Decide how many new members should be reached.*—When a study of the Sunday School possibilities is made, a church should decide how many new persons it will seek to reach. An enrolment goal and a worker enlistment goal will emerge from a study of the prospects by age groups. An average of at least one worker should be added for each ten new people who need to be reached for Bible study.

• *Motivate the workers to carry out outreach actions.*—The inner spirit of the worker—his love for Christ, his devotion to the church, his concern for unreached people, his belief in the Bible —prompts the worker to action. A sense of divine calling will lead a worker to establish a guiding purpose in carrying out his God-given, church-assigned responsibilities.

2. The Principle of Delegation

(1) *The principle stated.*—**Reaching prospects depends upon the effective delegation of responsibility to Sunday School workers.**

Most churches feel that *every* individual needs the inspiration, encouragement, and guidance that Bible study provides—preferably Bible study in a group. By accepting a place of service in the Sunday School, workers have, in effect, dedicated themselves to reaching every prospect for Bible study—including lost and un-churched persons who are prospects for the church. Sunday School administrative leaders need to recognize that the crucial aspect of outreach is at the point of delegation of responsibility. This concept of delegation, or "distributed responsibility," rests on a basic principle of administration.

(2) *The principle interpreted.*—Responsibility is appropriately delegated when the Sunday School organization makes every prospect for the church the responsibility of a particular unit in its Bible teaching program (including its extension activities). Such delegation magnifies, by units, the outreach task for prospects for the church as well as for Sunday School enrolment. It underscores the obligation for a class or department to reach a particular group of persons.

The key to delegation is the type of organizational pattern that is used. Organization should be democratic in that assignment of members and prospects is based on a fair and impartial plan. The pattern must reflect the basic educational principle of meeting the personal, spiritual needs of individuals. The organizational pattern should be reasonably compatible with that used by other churches, in order to facilitate cooperation and unity of purpose and to make the best use of available materials.

3. *The Principle of Grouping*

(1) *The principle stated.*—Reaching persons depends on using a grading and grouping plan that respects the individual's developmental stage and provides for annual promotion in all groups.

Every experience in life causes change in an individual. These changes characterize development through various life stages. Placing an individual in a compatible group not only recognizes the worth of the individual, but also places him in an atmosphere for Bible study that is planned to meet his life needs. As the individual grows and becomes older, he moves into the group designed to help meet his concerns and needs. Without a systematic plan for promotion, the grouping-grading system of the school becomes clogged and stagnant. Promotion protects what grouping provides.

(2) *The principle interpreted.*—The placement of members and the assignment of prospects on the basis of the above principle provide an environment conducive to growth. There are three prerequisites for proper observance of this principle: proper grading of the present Sunday School; correct classification of every new Sunday School member; and annual promotion for the entire Sunday School from the youngest to the oldest.

Promotion Day procedure may be simplified by moving to the new unit on the first Sunday in October, following promotion on the last Sunday in September. This procedure allows time for the visitation of all who are promoted, eliminates confusion and embarrassment in going to new places during the Sunday School hour, and, best of all, protects the Bible study time on Promotion Day.

4. *The Principle of Involvement of Learners*

In education the word "involve" means to draw in and engage as an active participant. Sustained, interested attendance at Sunday School rarely occurs apart from a satisfying involvement in learning. Spasmodic attendance results from meager involvement.

(1) *The principle stated.*—Reaching prospects depends upon the degree and quality of involvement which teacher and class members achieve in their Bible study.

(2) *The principle interpreted.*—The basis of our educational philosophy is found in God's Word. God created man with the capacity for thought and lifelong learning. The oldest adult prospect can be involved in stimulating learning experiences through the study of God's Word.

Learning is increased through group participation. The learner, studying in a group his own age, enjoys the experience as he becomes involved mentally and emotionally. Regular and faithful attendance then reinforces the learning process.

Most Sunday School workers would readily agree that thoughtful Bible Study is of primary importance to every individual. Yet many of these officers and teachers have unwittingly violated the principle of involvement. Three practical steps will serve as guidelines in securing the involvement of members in learning activities.

- *Interpret what involvement is.*—The strong emphasis on improved teaching must be accompanied by an equally important emphasis on learning. Effective group learning requires the involvement of the members in a personal search for truth and a mutual sharing of their discoveries, in line with the abilities and interests of the age group. Sunday School leaders bear the responsibility for helping teachers gain knowledge and skill in securing member involvement.

- *Offer training in the techniques of involvement.*—Teachers and department directors need help in planning learning activities that will involve members in thoughtful Bible study. They need training in how to use methods that secure involvement: discussing, Scripture searching and analysis, and other sound educational procedures. The teaching books in the Church Study Course offer excellent beginning help in this area. One thing is certain: the quality of member involvement will not surpass the quality of the planning and guidance which the teacher gives.

- *Show the relationship between involvement and sustained growth.*—Visitation to reach the prospects and teaching that involves them in purposeful Bible study are mutually dependent. Involvement in Bible study sustains the growth that visitation sets in motion. When teachers come to understand and observe this relationship, they will begin to make a truly significant contribution to reaching persons for Christ and Bible study.

5. The Principle of Visitation

(1) *The principle stated.*—**Reaching prospects depends upon the number and quality of visits made.**

Both church history and secular history reveal that the early churches employed visitation as their basic method of outreach. Visitation was an integral part of the church program because it was the essence of every effort to teach, preach, witness, and minister. The focal point of outreach visitation is the number and kind of visits made.

(2) *The principle interpreted.*—Outreach to the lost and unchurched is essentially a person-to-person relationship. The spirit of the visitor, his genuine interest in the person, and his consistency of effort will be contributing factors in reaching the person. Enrolment and attendance increase in proportion to the number of appropriate visits made. Through visitation, people can be influenced to be active participants in purposeful Bible study and, in fact, may be enrolled in Bible study by the visitor at the home or office. Visitation is a practical application of spiritual concern. When it is practiced regularly and faithfully by dedicated Sunday School workers, it becomes a declaration of how Christians love their Lord and love their fellowman.

If the pattern of visitation is to be followed continually and effectively, four actions are needed.

- Maintain a sustained emphasis on visitation.
- Follow a systematic plan of visitation.
- Assign responsibilities in visitation.
- Provide specific training in prospect visitation.
  Reporting results and sharing experiences also will strengthen visitation efforts.

6. The Principle of Organization

(1) *The principle stated.*—Reaching prospects depends upon the creation of new units designed to meet the growth potential at hand.

(2) *The principle interpreted.*—J. N. Barnette, in his book *The Pull of the People*, stated this principle: "New units grow faster, win more people to Christ, and provide more workers."

A Sunday School usually reaches its maximum growth or "saturation point" according to its organizational pattern. To continue to grow, new units of work must be started. This can be done in any one of the following ways:

- Select a teacher, provide a place to meet, give the teacher a list of names, and encourage him to build a class.
- Select a teacher, provide a place to meet, enlist a nucleus from an existing class or classes, give a list of prospects to the teacher, and encourage them to build a class. This has been done, but it leaves all of the other classes stationary except for replacing their losses to the new class.
- Select the required number of additional teachers, two or more, provide additional places to meet, divide the existing classes, assign lists of prospects, and encourage visitation. This is multiplying by division.
- The best way to set up new units is to regroup the entire school or department, adding to the total number of units. This means, of course, enlisting teachers, providing space and prospect lists, and launching visitation of prospects. It also means that every one of the classes will be new. The units will be small, but with intensified visitation growth will result in every unit. New units do grow faster; they win more people to Christ and put more people to work.

(Chap. 5, "Organizing for Enlargement," outlines in detail how this principle applies in a person-centered way to the work of the Bible teaching program.)

7. The Principle of Space and Facilities

(1) *The principle stated.*—Reaching prospects depends upon the expansion of space and other facilities as growth potential suggests the need.

Unless a church provides adequate space, that church could do everything else required to reach people and still fail to do so.

(2) *The principle interpreted.*—If a church fails to provide sufficient space, sustained growth is impossible. Assuming that growth potential is present, the amount of space and the kind of space provided will largely determine the number of people who will be reached and the quality of work that may be done with them. Space also will govern the kind of organization possible.

In 1962 a church was organized with 102 members. During the first year the church used many and varied meeting places in conducting its ministry: a grade public-school building, a savings and loan office, a basement of one member's home, a Lutheran church.

This new church occupied its first building, unfinished, one year later. Two years later the Sunday School enrolment reached 231 members. In 1965 the Sunday School enrolment reached 400 and climbed to 476 in 1966.

The second unit in the overall building plan was started in 1967 and was occupied in November of that year. Using the additional educational space, the enrolment continued to climb to 612 in 1967, 700 in 1968, and 800 in 1969.

As the church provided more space to reach more people, other areas of the life and work of the church showed corresponding growth. Though small in church membership, this church became one of the leaders in the state in additions by baptism and by letter. Other program organizations grew in enrolment and ministry.

Plans are well under way to begin the third educational unit. Provisions are planned to reach 1,500 persons for Bible study and for the preaching of the gospel.

Yes, provision of needed space will enable a church to extend its outreach and ministry.

8. The Principle of Relationship

(1) *The principle stated.*—Reaching prospects depends upon balanced, consistent, prayerful action in accordance with all the principles of growth.

(2) *The principle interpreted.*—The principles of outreach were not invented by man. They have been discovered through the experience of dedicated workers who sought the guidance of the Holy Spirit in regard to methods of work. They are practical, spiritual concepts that produce outstanding results when churches take the time and make the effort to apply them in a spirit of victory.

None of these principles is a "law unto itself." Rather, the successful application of any one of them is regulated by the successful application of other principles. When all the principles are applied in the proper proportion and the proper spirit and in full dependence upon the power of the Holy Spirit, they always bring gratifying results. When they are ignored or used only partially, the results are limited and disappointing.

A practical approach to observing this relationship includes three necessary actions:

- *Evaluate present application of these principles.*—The eight statements of principles of enlargement in this chapter may be used as a checklist to reveal those that are being used and those that are being ignored.
- *Make a deliberate beginning in the area of greatest need.*—The approach should be well planned and carefully communicated to the people. The suggestions for application of each of the eight principles already presented in this chapter will serve as guidelines for action.
- *Develop a long-range plan of action.*—Applying the principles on which enlargement is based is an ongoing responsibility of Sunday School leaders. The application of some principles, such as those relating to expansion, proportion, and balance, will require many months of planning and work. Others may take only a few

months. The best approach is a long-range plan with target dates when definite actions will be taken, and regular checkup.

II. Principles of Enlargement Applied

The principles of Sunday School enlargement must be applied to be effective. Practical, diligent steps must be taken in applying these principles.

1. *Know Your Possibilities*

The possibilities of any Sunday School include two groups of people: those already enrolled; and those not enrolled who are prospects. Prospects for the Sunday School of a Baptist church are:

Church members not enrolled in Sunday School
Baptists with their membership elsewhere
People in the community not enrolled in any Sunday School and
    not members of any church
People in the community belonging to other denominations but
    who prefer a Baptist church
People in the community who have no church preference

Many churches are enrolling these persons in Sunday School in their homes, their places of business, or school. Other churches obtain their names, addresses, and birth dates and assign them as prospects to classes and departments of the Sunday School. (To make a study of member possibilities for your Sunday School, use the "A Study of Bible Teaching Possibilities" sheet as given in chap. 5.)

2. *Enlarge the Organization*

This step simply means to provide enough classes and departments to reach the total possibilities. Refer to the guide for starting new units (chap. 5) for a discussion of this step.

3. *Provide the Needed Space*

Is all of the space being utilized, or can some adjustments be made? This is a good question. Each new class and department that is started will require a meeting place. (The pastor and/or director of the study of this book should have made a study of where the additional units might meet so that answers can be given when questions regarding space are raised by the people. See chap. 6.)

4. Enlist and Train the Workers

Workers are needed in three places as enlargement and improvement are considered. They are needed for *replacement*. The annual turnover of workers usually runs from 20 to 25 percent. Workers are needed for *conservation*. A study of most Sunday Schools will reveal a need for additional workers just to maintain present enrolments. Workers are needed for *expansion*. The principle of leadership and the principle of organization, as they are applied, will reveal the areas of need for additional workers.

Workers are available. Jesus encouraged us: "Pray ye therefore the Lord of the harvest, that he would send forth labourers into his harvest" (Luke 10:2).

The church that seeks out the workers needed and enlists them to accept places of leadership is obligated to help them carry out their tasks effectively. In large measure, numerical and spiritual growth depends upon the quality of Bible teaching that is done.

5. Go After the People

Visitation is perhaps the most important factor in the five-point growth formula. As the principles of growth are applied, all other steps may be taken, but without this step—continual visiting, going after new persons, following up on absentees—little or no growth can be expected. In Sunday School work, nothing produces more growth than making a crusade out of systematic, continual, and personal cultivation visitation by concerned Christians to the homes of persons not involved in regular Bible study. (Study chap. 8.)

4

IDENTIFYING
THE POSSIBILITIES
for Enlargement

SUNDAY SCHOOLS, like individuals, have personalities, needs, and characteristics of their own. However, all Sunday Schools are alike in that they can be enlarged and/or improved in their vision, ministry, and organization.

In chapter 3 we considered the principles by which Sunday Schools grow. We come now to relate these principles to the outreach responsibility of a church. We will seek to discover which of these principles apply to enlargement.

Every Sunday School must face the question: Do we really need to enlarge? The question can be answered fairly only when the principles discussed in chapter 3 are considered in the full knowledge of the total possibilities of the Sunday School.

Possibilities for enlargement should be considered from two points of view: (1) Do we have prospects for enlargement? (2) Do we have organizational possibilities for enlargement? The first question will be answered by a church as it carries out the prospect search outlined in this chapter or uses "ACTION: A Reach Out Enrollment Plan for Sunday School." (The second question will be answered in the study of chap. 5.)

I. Areas for Enlargement

An emphasis on Sunday School enlargement and improvement will focus attention on two areas. The first is within the physical facilities of the church. Enlargement will be necessary following prospect discovery and effective visitation or through use of "ACTION: A Reach Out Enrollment Plan for Sunday School."

The second possible area for enlargement does not require any of the physical facilities of the church building. It is beyond the church walls and is usually referred to as an extension of the church's ministry. This "beyond the church" ministry of the congregation is often overlooked.

1. *Possibilities for Enlargement Within the Church*

During the study of chapter 3, a church will be led to see how to apply the principles of growth. The need for new units will become clear through a study of the total possibilities of the Sunday School and by considering the principles set forth.

A further possibility for enlargement within a church is in the provision of weektime Bible study opportunities for those Sunday School prospects who cannot attend on Sunday but who can attend at another time. Such a ministry has possibilities of greatly extending the Bible study opportunity offered by any church. Classes for school-age children could be scheduled for one day each week following the regular public-school hours or on Saturday. A weektime class for adults may be scheduled before the working day begins, during the day, at an evening hour, or on Saturday.

Weektime Bible study opportunities need not be limited to persons who cannot attend a Sunday program. Some persons may want additional opportunity for Bible study during the week. A weektime class may be provided for those who teach on Sunday and are deprived of Bible study as members of a class.

Establishing a Cradle Roll to enroll the babies of members as soon as they are born will tie many families to the Bible study program.

2. Possibilities for Enlargement Beyond the Church

During the study of a tabulated report from the census or prospect search, the need for Bible study beyond the church building will be discovered. The extension activities director would lead in planning, directing, and coordinating the extension activities of the Bible teaching program. Further Bible study opportunities are offered through such ministries as Adults Away department, Cradle Roll department, fellowship Bible classes, new Sunday Schools, mission Bible classes, and special ministries to such groups as language groups, deaf persons, and the mentally retarded. (Mission action groups should be formed through WMU and Brotherhood to help a church meet opportunities in institutional ministries and language group ministries.)

Census workers will need to be properly instructed if prospects for enlargement beyond the church are to be discovered. Prospects should know of the church's interest in providing such ministries. Church leaders may be challenged to "stretch their minds" in planning for this type of outreach.

II. Purposes of a Prospect Search

A hunter aims the gun at a target. The golfer sights a line toward the cup on the green. The retail merchant directs his "sales pitch" to capture the interest of a potential customer. Each of these has an object in his line of vision. The most effective witness by a New Testament church will be that which aims toward a definite object. In fact, a church cannot approach intelligently the performance of its witness without defining the objects of its aim. It must have information about the people who are in need of its ministry.

When Jesus saw the multitudes, he was moved with compassion; he ministered to them as individuals. There are multitudes of people around our churches, but they remain impersonal multitudes until we see them as individuals. The objective of any prospect search is to identify individuals with their various spiritual needs. This axiom dates back to the earliest days of vigorous

Sunday School work in Southern Baptist churches. Arthur Flake stated it this way: "Know your possibilities."

A prospect search may serve many important purposes:

1. *To Discover Unsaved People and Inactive Church Members*

The character and pattern of today's society allow people to "get lost" from the church. On the average, one out of every five families has moved within the last year; and one out of every two has moved within the last five years. A scheduled, recurring prospect search is necessary to locate persons who need the ministry of a church.

2. *To Locate Places for Missions or New Sunday Schools*

The only reliable way to determine the needs for new Sunday Schools and new churches is to discover the unreached people living in a given area and to decide whether they can best be reached through a mission or a Sunday School.

3. *To Accept Opportunities for Witnessing*

Contacts made during a prospect search provide the searcher with opportunities for Christian witness. Many persons, as they work with a more experienced witness, will, for the first time in their lives, feel and express concern for the spiritual welfare of others.

When one person asks about the spiritual welfare of another with the purpose of helping to meet his needs, he can be witnessing. When a census is conducted with sensitive concern for human need, it reveals the heartbeat of a church. Such efforts convey the impression that the church involved is trying to be a church and to carry out the ministry assigned to it by Christ.

III. Types of Prospect Search

There are many ways of finding prospects. The type search employed will be determined on the basis of need, available resources, and other pertinent factors.

1. Inside Census

Any church can take an inside census, and should do so regularly. Such a census includes using prospect file cards, Form 5, for (1) all church members and others in their families not enrolled in Sunday School; (2) church and Sunday School visitors who have registered their attendance; (3) those not enrolled in Sunday School who have some member of the family on the Sunday School roll, or in some organization of the church. While not technically part of an inside census, VBS records reveal many names of persons not enrolled in Bible study.

The inside census pursues those who have already had some contact with the church. Home contacts may be required, but a minimum of organization is needed as a church seeks to discover those who are likely to be the most responsive to its ministry, those who already have contact with the church.

2. Church Community Religious Census

The church community census is an organized search of the area being served (or that should be served) by a church. It is one of the most effective ways for a church to discover its prospects. When a community census is conducted at least annually, it provides new and current information for the visitation ministry of the church. This census can be conducted through one of various projects, to be determined by the purpose to be served and the conditions which govern the action.

• *Door-to-door canvass.*—Usually the most valuable census is a door-to-door canvass of the community. This approach speaks out in strong testimony for the church conducting the census. It provides firsthand information on entire families that is usually reliable.

• *Telephone canvass.*—There has been a growing interest among churches in the telephone approach to community census. The plan permits the canvass of three or four times as many families as would be possible in a door-to-door census. Also, the telephone canvass can use workers who would not be available in a door-to-door effort—for example, those confined to their homes for various reasons. When the area to be covered is large and the number of available workers is limited, the telephone census may be the wise approach. It would permit a total canvass of the area and provide usable statistical information for a study of needs for additional churches. This type of survey demands the utmost tact on the part of the canvasser.

• *Baby hunt.*—A search of the community for new babies is an excellent method to discover prospects. Hospital reports, newspaper birth announcements, and alert church members are some of the sources of information about families with new babies. Many Baptist churches have their own special ministry to such families. This ministry is directed toward the parents but comes on the occasion of the discovery of the child. The timeliness of this interest shown by the church and the object of the interest makes a baby hunt a popular activity in most communities. Such a hunt can be conducted by a Cradle Roll department or even by an Adult class or department.

• *"Wanted" listing.*—A particular group in the church—such as an Adult department, a WMU circle, or a Brotherhood group—may be asked to fill out cards giving information on prospects they know. Slips for this purpose may be prepared by the church. This approach could be used monthly or quarterly, selecting a different group each time. Names for the wanted list may include unchurched neighbors, fellow employees, business associates, fellow club members, schoolmates, teachers, or other persons met in the course of a normal day—milkmen, mailmen, beauty operators, and others.

• *Newcomer lists.*—Prospects may be discovered from lists of newcomers to the community. Such lists may be secured from a community hostess, Welcome Wagon, utility company, and other sources.

• *Updating a church community religious census.*—Since taking a religious census involves considerable expenditure of time and effort in planning and conducting, churches should fully use the information obtained. One way to make better use of the census is to keep the census cards current by regularly updating them. This approach is particularly adaptable to the People Search Family Card. Information on these cards can be updated by the following plan:

- Arrange the cards of a previous census in the order of their street addresses. This may be in a master file or it may be in the assignment packets used during the census. Be sure there is a card for every house (or family unit) in the area being worked.
- Telephone each family to verify the information received during the last census. A street address directory may be used to determine whether the same family is living at a given address. Correct the card on the basis of information obtained in the telephone interview. Place the current date on the card before returning it to the file.
- When there has been a change in residence at a given address, a new card may be filled out to record the information gained in the telephone interview. A worker may be asked to visit that address, thus providing opportunity for the face-to-face approach in securing the information.
- A personal visit will need to be made to families who have no telephone, or who have a telephone with an unlisted number.

This approach to census information assumes that a card will be filled out on every family in the community. The "churched" family may be encouraged to provide the information requested by the canvasser when they learn that the canvasser's church is attempting to keep a file card on every family in the community, that no attempts at proselyting will be made, and that information will be shared with their church preference. It would seem wise for any church to have a plan for frequent updating of its census in order to keep up with the community it serves.

Updating the census should be done at least once a year and sometimes more often. The mobility of a community and the availability of workers for such a project would be determining factors. Assignments for keeping census cards up to date may be made to the church staff, if there are sufficient staff members. The outreach director working through the department outreach leaders would keep the prospect information up to date. Updating a previous census requires a fairly recent card file from which to work. It also requires regular attention if the information is to be kept current. However, the plan is very workable and is being carried out effectively in some communities. A complete census of the area is not necessary in order to begin the plan. Updating may be done for a few streets covered in a recent census. This will allow the church to cover other streets on the next census and add these to the file for continuous, regular updating. Conceivably, a church would spend several months completing a census of the church community, but would need to continue updating the census cards. Thus, the church would keep itself informed of changes in the area previously covered by the census.

IV. Planning the Prospect Search

Planning for a prospect search may involve a number of people in the church and be carried out over a period of several weeks. Necessary steps are listed in the order in which they should be considered by church leaders.

1. *Determine the Type Search to Be Conducted*

The first step in planning for a prospect search should be selection of the plan to be followed. Purposes to be served, available calendar time, resources, and possible involvement of workers will be determining factors in making the selection.

2. *Set Aside Calendar Time*

Adequate time should be allowed for the necessary preparation. This may involve a few days or a period of several months for persons who do the planning and preparation for the project. It will take time to secure the supplies, prepare the assignments, enlist and train the workers, and prepare for tabulating the results. The actual dates for the survey will usually involve only one or two or three days. A baby hunt might be completed in one day, whereas the church community religious census might require three days.

Some churches have found that census taking can begin on Saturday and continue through Sunday for a good coverage. Others take a census during the period Friday to Sunday. The traditional Sunday afternoon has proved to be a very poor time in some areas because of sports activities, family outings, and other activities.

September and October are among the most desirable times to conduct a prospect search. This date puts the church in touch with new people at the beginning of a Sunday School year and affords the leadership maximum time in attempting to minister to needs. The coming of a new Sunday School year will often bring a change in leadership and a reassignment of prospects, thus setting up a new relationship between director or teacher and prospect. The fall months usually find families settling down from summer activities and getting organized for the school year. They may be more receptive to involvement in Bible study at this time of year.

3. Order Necessary Supplies

The following supplies are needed and may be secured from a Baptist Book Store:

(1) *People Search Assignment Packet.*—Order a quantity equal to the attendance divided by five.

(2) *People Search Family Card.*—Order four times the Sunday morning attendance for telephone survey and three times the attendance for the door-to-door survey.

(3) *Prospect File Card, Form 5.*—Order a quantity six times the Sunday morning attendance.

(4) *Prospect Visitation Assignment and Report, Form 120.*—Order a quantity eight times the Sunday morning attendance.

4. Enlist Necessary Workers

The pastor, general Sunday School director, outreach director, or some other qualified person selected by the church should serve as prospect search chairman. He will direct the total activity in this project and lead in the selection of other census workers. A worker should be enlisted to canvass each assignment. Young adults and many teen-agers make good canvassers. Workers also will be needed to prepare the assignments and to tabulate the results.

Enlistment of census takers should begin about a month before the date for the search. The Sunday School organization is well suited to do the enlisting. The following schedule may be considered:

- On Sunday, four weeks before the search, sign up the general Sunday School officers.
- On Sunday, three weeks before the search, ask general Sunday School officers to enlist participation of department directors and department officers.
- On Sunday, two weeks before the search, ask department officers to enlist class teachers and workers in the children's departments.
- On Sunday, one week before the search, ask teachers in the appropriate age groups to secure involvement of class officers and class members.

This approach to worker enlistment allows time (about one month) and involves a large number of people. Both of these factors contribute to successful enlistment. If all of the Sunday School officers and teachers were enlisted, they would number about 10 percent of the Sunday School enrolment. This total is a desirable goal to set for worker enlistment. Some types of prospect search would not need to involve so many workers, and some modification could be made in the approach to enlistment.

5. Prepare Census Assignments

Assignments should be prepared early enough to be ready for distribution following the training sessions for workers. Perhaps the general Sunday School officers enlisted four weeks before the date of the search, or other workers, enlisted early for the purpose, could prepare the assignments.

A People Search Assignment Packet would be used for almost any type of prospect search. Space is available on the face of the envelope for a specific designation of the territory to be worked. A wise plan for door-to-door canvassing is to assign all four sides of a city block (when the number of units is reasonable) to one canvasser. This method allows him to finish at the location of his car. He is instructed to work around the block, taking every house, and not to cross a street.

Other information on the envelope should include a name and phone number the canvasser may call should a need arise while he is out conducting the search. The envelope has a space for the worker to fill out his name and phone number. This information may be used by those processing the cards if a question arises about information reported. The envelope also calls for an assignment number to be used in keeping a record of all outgoing assignments, thus insuring that each one is returned. For identification, the number also is to be placed on each card in that assignment. This information will be used in refiling the cards after processing. Refiling is essential in the event that a church plans to update the cards according to the plan already discussed.

If the People Search Family Card is used, place a number of cards in each envelope equal to the estimated number of family units in the assignment. Since the number of needed cards cannot be easily determined, a few extra cards should be included in every assignment envelope. Include sharpened pencils, church bulletins, and visitation cards or folders. Census Taker Nameplates also are available from Baptist Book Stores.

A reasonable assignment for each canvasser in a door-to-door census would be about twenty-five units. Twenty might be more acceptable in some rural areas, and thirty might be assigned in some metropolitan areas. An assignment for a telephone canvasser could include up to one hundred family units.

Assignments should be numbered and arranged in the order of importance—that is areas which can be worked later will be assigned last. The "prime" area, determined by whatever consideration those making the assignments care to use, should be the first to be worked.

6. Instruct the Workers

The church census chairman is responsible for training the workers. He may conduct the necessary training session, or he may select someone to give instructions.

Each worker should know why the prospect search is being conducted and the possible values to be obtained from it. Each canvasser should know how to make the approach and how to fill out the information card accurately and completely. To permit canvassers to go out without instructions is a mistake.

Two types of training are necessary:

(1) *Training for the canvasser.*—He should have the instructions on the assignment envelope explained to him. He must have in mind a description of the territory he is to canvass and the boundaries to be respected. Each canvasser must be familiar with the card form being used and understand the reasons for each question to be asked. The following list of instructions relates to the People Search Family Card.

- Canvass every home (or apartment) described on the face of your People Search Assignment Packet. Fill out on the People Search Family Card information on the religious affiliation of each family (unless otherwise instructed). Secure information on *each family member* from unchurched families only.

- You may begin your canvassing as soon as you have received your instructions in training.
- Saturday is the best day of the week for canvassing.
- Note when the assignment is to be completed and plan your work accordingly. Assignments will require an average of two to three hours to complete.
- In most cases the packet committee has already placed the name, address, zip code, and phone number on the card. If this has not been done, include in each interview questions to secure this information.
- Leave the first column on the left open for processing purposes.
- Reserve the top line for the husband, the second for the wife, and subsequent lines for the children in order of descending age.
- Secure information on the persons granting the interview first, then seek information on other family members.
- Ask general questions such as, "What church does your family attend in the community?" Only the religious affiliation of the family is recorded on the card if they are members of another church or Sunday School. An additional question can determine if there are exceptions to the "family" answer.
- The "attendance" column is important. It is the basis for classifying individuals as prospects or not prospects.
- Secure date of birth (age) and school grade. These are necessary for making proper visitation assignments at a later date. Begin with the youngest child and move up to the adults. Date of birth is more readily given than a request for age. If ages are given, mark out "date of birth" and "month" and insert an "A" under month in column 8.
- Do not ask the question, "Are you a Christian?" Some people will respond affirmatively to the question, meaning, "I'm not a Jew, a Hindu, or a Moslem." The response may have no reference to the person's relationship to Jesus

Christ as personal Lord and Savior. You may best answer this question yourself following the interview. Base your answer on the response to question of church attendance. A later church visitor can determine more accurately the person's spiritual condition.

• Rate the family as prospects for your church either good, possible, or poor. Determine the rating on the basis of the person's attitude and cooperation. Do not rate families on the basis of felt need.

• Check for accuracy the cards you have filled out. Do not return the "not at home" cards. Keep and try to complete them within the next few days.

• Return the cards in person, if possible, since those processing the cards may need to ask for clarification of some points.

(2) *Training for processors.*—After the information has been obtained by the canvassers, it must be processed. This involves determining the unchurched, preparing visitation forms, and refiling the census cards. (The procedure is discussed under Section VI, "Processing.")

V. Conducting the Prospect Search

When the date for the prospect search has arrived, workers will begin to function according to their prior instructions.

A church may need to have a transportation committee to get canvassers to and from their assignments. Provision should be made for small children; otherwise, some workers cannot serve.

1. *Check Out Assignments*

Each canvasser will take an assignment to work. Some may prefer to work in pairs if door-to-door visits are made, but each would be asked to accept a separate assignment.

Assignments will be distributed after the training session for canvassers. A receipt form will be filled out for each assignment, allowing the chairman to know when all have been returned. If unexpected circumstances prevent a worker from completing his assignment, then the chairman may have it reassigned.

When door-to-door canvassing is done, a large map of the community placed on the wall will prove most helpful. Each canvasser must understand the boundaries of his assignment.

2. Insist That Workers Follow Instructions

Each canvasser will accept his assignment and follow instructions given during the training session. Any variation may limit the usefulness of the census.

3. Check In the Assignments

A time and place should be designated for the return of completed assignments. The report form on which the assignment was noted when it was given out will now be completed. This step is essential for efficiency in processing the information.

VI. Processing the Results of the Search

Information secured in any prospect search should be immediately prepared for use by the church. For any type census card, the processing would include the same steps:

1. Coding the Cards

Selected workers should carefully study each name that appears on each card. On the basis of information collected by the canvasser, decision is made as to whether the individual is a prospect. The letter "P" (for prospect) is placed in the space provided for coding in the margin opposite each name. Prospects include: (1) persons not enrolled in any Sunday School; (2) persons not members of any church; (3) persons not members of a local church; (4) those who indicate they seldom or never attend Sunday School or church.

Every card bearing the name of any prospect is placed in a stack separate from the "churched" cards. If the family card is used, then any card with one or more prospect names on it would go in the "prospect stack" for transfer to Prospect File Card, Form 5.

2. Preparing Enrolment Prospect Visitation Forms

Remember, Prospect Visitation Assignment and Report, Form 120, should be prepared for every prospect. In projects where churches work cooperatively in a community or associational census, names of all prospects should be shared with the participating churches, either by means of duplicate cards or duplicated lists. Each church should prepare its own Form 120.

Preparation of the visitation form is the objective of the processing step. This work can be done by anyone who can type (or write legibly). Simply take cards from the "prospect" stack and transfer the necessary information to Form 120. The transfer usually is made in a processing center set up at a church office for this purpose.

3. Refiling Cards

The final phase of the processing step is filing the census card for future use. If the updating plan already described is to be followed, the card should be filed by census assignment. Other possible use of the cards might dictate the method for filing them, such as alphabetically or by age groupings. Other help on securing and using prospect information may be found in the Convention Press book *People Search Guide,* available at Baptist Book Stores.

VII. Using the Information Received

All of the work of preparing, conducting, and processing the prospect search has been for one or more of these purposes: to enrol prospects in Sunday School; to win the unsaved to Christ; to lead the unaffiliated Baptists to unite with the local church; and to identify those who need some ministry of the church.

These purposes may be accomplished by (1) enlisting persons in the existing church organizations; (2) expanding the existing organizations to provide for more people; (3) starting a new mission or church; or (4) taking some other ministry action to individuals who have special need.

A church will proceed in a deliberate way to reach those prospects discovered in the search. The remaining chapters of this book discuss the plans a church may follow in providing a ministry to the unchurched.

5

ORGANIZING
for Enlargement

ORGANIZATION always needs to be as simple as possible yet still to be effective. *Working in Sunday School*, compiled by A. V. Washburn and Donald F. Trotter tells about organization. Organizing the Sunday School for enlargement requires an understanding of leaders and members and what they want to accomplish for Christ in outreach. Organization in the context of this chapter means effectively relating members, leaders, prospects, and resources so that the task "reach persons for Christ and church membership" will be accomplished.

I. Responsibility for Organization

The words "Christian initiative" are key words in leading a church in Sunday School enlargement. Some persons or groups of persons, must have the vision, must feel the need, must see the possibilities, and must understand the process to a degree that will motivate organization for enlargement. Somebody has to "get the ball rolling." Someone must be brave enough to move out ahead. Someone must "dare to do." Who in a church is responsible for organization? Who logically takes the initiative? This is an important question, and it needs a clear answer. Certainly organization is a shared responsibility.

1. The Responsibility of the Church Staff

(1) *The pastor.*—Because of his role as "under shepherd of the flock," the pastor is in a logical position to lead the church to enlarge its Bible teaching program. This action is based on his conviction that the Sunday School offers an effective way of promoting much of the work of the church. It is the program organization to which a church logically assigns the task of reaching persons for Christ and the church. A pastor who yearns to reach more people for Christ should exercise his leadership ability in leading the Sunday School to enlarge its outreach to the unchurched.

(2) *The minister of education.*—When a church has this staff member, he is given many of the responsibilities in leading a Sunday School to carry out detailed outreach actions. He will recognize that basically the church will use its Sunday School to involve persons in the life and work of the church. To this end he will lead his church to start new classes and departments and will see that they are assigned specific prospects to visit, cultivate, enlist, and teach. In this way he will help his church to accomplish New Testament objectives.

(3) *Other staff members.*—In larger churches there are other staff members devoting a majority of their time to work with children, youth, or adults. Each of these staff members will work through the pastor, minister of education, and Sunday School director in leading a particular age group to reach their growth potential.

2. The Responsibility of Other Church Officers

Volunteer leaders elected by the congregation are responsible for taking initiative in organization and reorganization. The person most clearly identified in this role for the Sunday School is the director. In a small Sunday School, the director and the pastor working together will be the persons to study all angles of the situation and to recommend enlargement action to the church for approval. If the director has responsibilities for a large Sunday School, it is appropriate for him to have an outreach director to assist him. This officer then becomes the chief resource person for enlargement recommendations.

Initiative also must issue from other volunteers elected as Sunday School leaders. Next in order are the department directors. These persons have easiest access to records, are most acquainted with the operation of a department, and can most quickly observe the needs for reorganization. If department directors and outreach leaders understand the philosophy for enlargement, the need for creating new units, and the principle of leadership, they can greatly assist in outreach as it is conceived in the New Testament.

Class teachers must take equal initiative if healthy organization is to be maintained. When a teacher is possessive of his members, does not want new units to be created from his large class, refuses to commend promotion to his members, or fails to lead his class members to concern for the unreached regardless of who they are, that teacher is hindering Sunday School growth. He too must understand the Christian philosophy of enlargement.

It is important for the outreach leader, group leaders and other class members to understand the enlargement principles and their application. The chain of responsibility for outreach runs unbroken from the church staff to members of the class.

3. The Responsibility of the Church

When the responsible persons have taken the initiative for proposing organizational adjustments, their recommendations must be considered, evaluated, and acted upon before actual reorganization takes place.

The class member not often voices such recommendations, but his awareness of their need and his willingness to adjust are desirable for successful reorganization.

When a teacher sees he can meet the needs of his members and reach more of his prospects by a change in organization in his class or department, he should speak to his department director concerning the matter. Certainly the alert department director will help the Sunday School director or the outreach director to be aware of organizational needs.

In all likelihood the initiative for stirring up awareness of the need for enlargement and reorganization will come from the Sunday School director and the outreach director. They will consult with department directors and teachers and produce specific recommendations for the creation of new units and other adjustment of organization conducive to enlarging the Sunday School. These persons, however, need to have a place for their recommendations to be heard and evaluated.

(1) *The Sunday School council.*—The most adequate sounding board for proposed organizational adjustments can be the Sunday School council (the general officers and department directors). When council members can see the whole picture in a unified manner, and can recommend every element of organizational enlargement, the school can expect to adjust more rapidly and congenially than otherwise it might.

(2) *The church council.*—The Sunday School cannot reorganize without affecting other organizations in the church, however. It is essential, therefore, that other persons of leadership responsibility be aware of, and concur in, the projected changes. The logical place for the discussion of such matters is the church council. This group should consider sympathetically any recommendations coming from the Sunday School council. A spirit of togetherness among the leaders who comprise the church council concerning the recommendations does much to strengthen the spirit and assure victory for the adjustments proposed.

(3) *The congregation.*—Within the understanding of Baptist polity, the ultimate responsibility for all church matters is in the hands of the fellowship, or the congregation. As a church takes action on recommendations of the Sunday School council or

church council, organizational adjustments can still be heard and made by the congregation. This is a freedom to be observed in a church.

If the explorations experienced in a Sunday School enlargement campaign produce evidence requiring regrouping the entire organization, the recommendations may be presented directly to the congregation to be considered at its discretion.

It is sufficient to say that a church is responsible under the leadership of the Lord for an orderly arrangement of its leaders and members in relationship to one another according to their assigned responsibilities in carrying out its program.

II. Extent of Organization

Every time a church takes steps to enlarge its Bible teaching program, certain questions must be asked and answered: When should the organization be changed? How much should it be changed? At what points must it be changed? How much can the organization be changed? Will the proposed reorganization be conducive to improved quality of Bible teaching and more effective performance of its members? In order to answer some of these questions, a number of steps can be taken by those who lead out in the reorganization.

1. Study the Present Organization

A basic tool for use in determining the points of need in enlargement reorganization is the chart "A Study of Bible Teaching Possibilities." This will provide information concerning the number of units now in the organization, the present enrolment in each unit, and the number of leaders now provided for each. This chart also proposes the enrolment ceiling of departments and classes and the suggested ratio of workers to members. Thus it provides a quick comparison between the existing organization and the pattern suggested for an ideal organization.

Study of the chart provides an evaluation of the existing organization. However, such evaluation should be extended beyond the comparison of the figures on the chart. The following also should be considered: (1) Is the organization as it now exists functioning smoothly? (2) Has the pattern undergirded outreach and numerical growth? (3) Is there an appreciable slowdown in existing growth over the past several years? (4) Have any of the present units become static? (5) Does the organization as it now exists provide an efficient base for applying the principles of growth?

When the answers to the above questions are predominantly negative in nature, they indicate a need for adjustment in organization, even though ceiling enrolments for the units have not been reached.

2. Study the Possibilities of Enlargement

The plans for the identification of possibilities for enlargement (chap. 4) make it simple to enter on the chart the number of prospects for every unit and division of the Sunday School. Proceed by adding the number of persons presently enrolled in each unit to the number of prospects that have been identified as possibilities for enlargement. Judge this enlarged figure by the department and class enrolment ceiling and ratio of workers that could be used in a revised organization. When this has been done by every person willing to study the possibilities, there will emerge a pattern of organization larger and more challenging than would have been imagined by most leaders in the organization. When this has been done, there will be no room for persons to say: "We do not need to make any adjustments. We are doing all right as we are"; or "We can't grow."

At this point a study of organization can take on a quality far exceeding organizational patterns and units for growth. With the picture of total possibilities before him, the spiritual leader tests his faith. The person with vision can see the "big picture." Those who have thought that no enlargement could take place can see it as not only possible but imperative. This is where the doubter can become the dreamer. Resolute optimism can prevail, measured by living statistics and gauged by the faith and courage of the group seeking to enlarge.

A STUDY OF BIBLE TEACHING POSSIBILITIES

Date of Study _____, "Now" Date (Cols. 7, 12, 17) _____, "Future" Date (Cols. 8, 13, 18) _____

Age Groups	Pupil Possibilities			Departments					Classes						Workers			
	1 Enrolled	2 Prospects	3 Total Possibilities	4 Enrollment Ceiling	5 Have Now	6 Additional Needed	7 Organize Now	8 Organize Future	9 Enrollment Ceiling	10 Have Now	11 Additional Needed	12 Organize Now	13 Organize Future	14 Ratio Workers to Members	15 Have Now	16 Additional Needed	17 Enlist Now	18 Enlist Future
Preschool Division																		
Cradle Roll				50										1-6				
Department I (B-1)				12					x	x	x	x	x	1-4				
(1)				12					x	x	x	x	x	1-4				
(2)				20					x	x	x	x	x	1-4				
(3)				20					x	x	x	x	x	1-4				
(4)				25					x	x	x	x	x	1-5				
(5)				25					x	x	x	x	x	1-5				
Children's Division																		
Department I (6) G1				30					x	x	x	x	x	1-7				
(7) G2				30					x	x	x	x	x	1-7				
(8) G3				30					x	x	x	x	x	1-7				
(9) G4				30					x	x	x	x	x	1-7				
(10) G5				30					x	x	x	x	x	1-7				
(11) G6				30					x	x	x	x	x	1-7				
Youth Division																		
Department I (12) G7				50					10					x				
(13) G8				50					10					x				
(14) G9				50					10					x				
(15) G10				60					15					x				
(16) G11				60					15					x				
(17) G12				60					15					x				

	College	Single (18-29)	Married (18-29)	Married (30-)	( )	( )	( )	(-up)	Weektime	Homebound	Adults Away	Fellowship Bible Classes	New Sunday Schools	Weekday Bible Study	Special Education	General Officers	Totals
Adult Division																	
	125	125	125	125	125	125	125	125	125	75	75				20		
												x	x	x		x	x
												x	x	x		x	x
												x	x			x	x
	25	25	25	25	25	25	25	25	25	8	6	25	x		x	x	
													x		x	x	
															x	x	
															x	x	
	x	x	x	x	x	x	x	x	x	x	x	x	x	x	1-4	x	

3. *Determine the Need for New Units, Now and in the Future*

Many churches do not have enough classes and departments to reach all, or even a sizable portion, of their possibilities. The following procedures may be used in planning for new units:

(1) *Consider the trends in present units.*—While suggested maximum enrolments furnish guidelines, other variables—such as the abilities, time, experience, and dedication of the workers—affect the growth. However, a careful analysis of the enrolment and the average attendance, along with the attendance pattern of each member, will provide some insights. If the average attendance and the enrolment are still increasing, the unit has growth potential. If the enrolment is static, while the average attendance has reached a peak and leveled off and the absentee list is uniformly the same, then a change in organization is needed. In many cases, the age range of the unit should be narrowed and one or more additional units organized.

(2) *Determine the possibilities.*—The term "possibilities" refers to present enrolment plus all the prospects. Through a thorough religious census, a church may learn how many prospects it has. The information obtained in the census should be grouped for effective sharing with proper classes and departments. Then the number of prospects for each age group should be added to the enrolment. The totals are the possibilities for Sunday School enrolment for each year.

(3) *Analyze the organizational needs in relation to possibilities.*—A recommended organizational pattern for a Sunday School will serve as a rule-of-thumb guide in determining how many new units are needed. (See "A Study of Bible Teaching Possibilities," p. 60.) By comparing the possibilities to the present enrolment, Sunday School leaders can gain a working estimate of how many classes and departments their school needs to add and can pinpoint the areas of greatest need. A school may need two or more units for some age groups, even though the total possibilities are less than the ceiling suggested in the chart.

(4) *Give priority to areas of greatest need.*—Probably no church can provide immediately all the units of organization it needs in order to reach all its possibilities. But every church can make a beginning at closing the gap between the ideal and the actual.

Two factors seem to indicate that the pressing need in most Sunday Schools is for more classes and departments for adults. First, the majority of all Sunday School prospects are adults. (Percentages vary from one community to another.) Second, the enlargement needed throughout the school will be impossible until additional adults are reached and some of these are trained as workers.

Balance in Sunday School work is essential to the well-being of the school and the health of the church. To test the balance in your Sunday School, complete the following chart.

Age Group	Percentages Population	Percentages Sunday School Enrolment	Age Group	Percentages Population	Percentages Sunday School Enrolment
Preschool Children	10–12 14–16		Youth Adult	9–10 62–64	

(5) *Add new units each year.*—The best approach to enlargement is to add some classes and departments annually at promotion time, if the number of prospects warrants this. This procedure provides a systematic approach to keeping the school growing and offsets the problem of saturation. Some schools also organize new units in the early spring months, while there is still time for the unit to get under way before vacation time.

(6) *Continually interpret enlargement as an expression of concern.*—Successful enlargement hinges on spiritual motivation. Christians should look upon enlargement of the Sunday School as a practical approach to sharing Christ's concern for the unreached and to reaching prospects for the church. Enlargement is leading more persons to receive the ministry of our Lord.

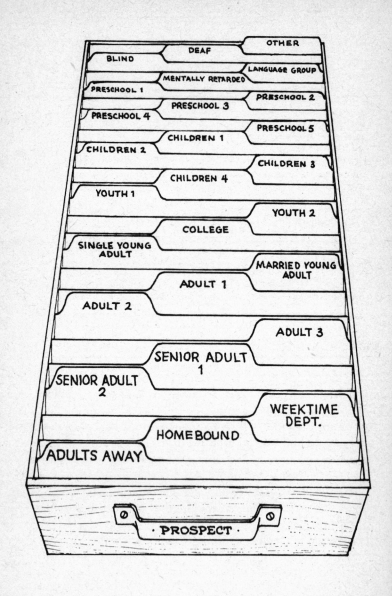

PROSPECT VISITATION ASSIGNMENT AND REPORT

NAME_____DATE_____

(IF UNDER 17 YEARS OF AGE GIVE PARENTS NAME)_____

RESIDENCE ADDRESS_____PHONE_____

BUSINESS ADDRESS_____PHONE_____

DATE OF BIRTH. MONTH_____DAY_____YEAR_____CHRISTIAN?_____

CHURCH MEMBER?_____MEMBER OF WHAT CHURCH?_____

WHERE_____

SPECIAL INFORMATION FOR VISITOR_____

DATE ASSIGNED _____   CLASS
                                                OR UNION_____
☐ S.S. ☐ T.U. DEPARTMENT_____

☐ MUSIC   CHOIR OR DIRECTOR _____

☐ W.M.U. ☐ BROTHERHOOD_____

VISITED BY	RESULTS OF VISITS	DATE VISITED

PLEASE VISIT, RECORD RESULTS AND RETURN SLIP PROMPTLY

FORM 120. CODE 4388-04. BROADMAN SUPPLIES, NASHVILLE, TENN. PRINTED IN U. S. A.

GUIDE FOR STARTING NEW UNITS

Groupings Involved		Class Needed for Every	Department Can Be Started When There Exists	New Units This Church Needs	
				Classes	Depts.
Adult:					
	Men	10 to 25	⎡ I class for men ⎤		
	Women	10 to 25	⎣ I class for women ⎦		
Young Adult:					
	Men	8 to 20	⎡ I class for men ⎤		
	Women	8 to 20	⎣ I class for women ⎦		
Youth:					
	Boys	8 to 10	⎡ I class for boys ⎤		
	Girls	8 to 10	⎣ I class for girls ⎦		
Children:					
	Boys	6 to 8	⎡ I class for boys ⎤		
	Girls	6 to 8	⎣ I class for girls ⎦		
Children			4 to 30 enrolled		
Preschool			4 to 25 enrolled		
Preschool			4 to 20 enrolled		

4. Acknowledge Any Limitations the Church May Face

In most cases, when the above procedure is followed, the enlarged organization called for will be greater than the church can provide. There will be a number of limiting factors to overcome.

(1) *Space limitations.*—Another factor that obviously limits the ideal in enlargement organization relates to the space available. Here again, before spirits are dampened and a retreat in enlargement plans begins, a review of chapter 6 on providing space and equipment for enlargement is recommended. Most churches can find some space for enlargement. When organization dictates a requirement for major space adjustments, this may stimulate the action required by the church to buy adjoining property or to initiate plans for the construction of new space.

(2) *Financial considerations.*—Finances may be another limiting factor in enlargement. The primary reason for enlargement is to involve persons in the study of God's Word to the end that they may know Christ as Savior and Lord, and follow him in life. When a church makes this purpose foremost in its program, the results are further available finances required for enlargement, and for every other phase of Christian stewardship support.

(3) *Lack of concern.*—A church also may face limitations because of the attitudes of the members and their lack of knowledge concerning the significance of enlargement efforts. For the improvement of such attitudes and for the supplying of the right vision concerning enlargement, this book has been prepared.

5. Be Guided by the Principles Which Determine Growth

As a further step in evaluating the proposed enlargement organization, make another review of the principles of growth (chap. 3). Prayerfully answer the following questions:

• Are we willing to propose an organization that will make possible the delegating of responsibility so that every unreached person in the community is the responsibility of someone in Sunday School?

- Is the organization we are about to propose such that it will provide a ratio of enrolment to workers conducive to growth?
- Are we proposing an organization that will make possible planning and supervising an effective program of visitation?
- Does the new organization being considered propose the creation of new units at the places where they are most vitally needed? Do the new units provide an adequate means for effective grouping of members?
- Does the proposal for reorganization make clear what space and facilities are needed? Has a study of space been made? Is the church willing to provide space for adequate organization?
- In the proposals for reorganization, does there appear to be a degree of balance maintained among the units? For example, if more units are proposed in the Children's Division, is there a balance of new units proposed for the parents of the children?
- Does the reorganization proposed make possible a specific grouping-grading of the members in a pattern that can be maintained effectively through an annual promotion plan?
- Do the new units envision the grouping of persons in an environment conducive to an effective teaching-learning situation?
- Is that which is being proposed of such a nature that it will encourage dedication on the part of officers and teachers? Are the units of such a character and size that officers and teachers feel that they can assume the responsibility called for?
- Is the organization being considered of such a nature that each one of the principles previously cited can be applied?

When the preceding questions have been answered in the affirmative, effective proposals for enlargement are near at hand.

6. *In Faith, Agree on the New Units to Be Added*

The application of the principles of growth provides the pattern of organization. But the degree of their application is determined by the vision and faith of Sunday School leaders in recommending enlargement to the church. Items 1 and 2 in the procedures suggested in this section produce a vision of what the Sunday School organization should aim for. Items 3 and 4 of this section temper the ideal with the practical. Judgment balanced with vision and faith produces an organization that will glorify God in outreach for lost and needy persons.

When, by prayer and study, the best judgments are reached, it is time to write down specific recommendations for church consideration. Identify every point where reorganization should take place, and describe the picture of the units as they are proposed for the new organization. This written recommendation will become the major section of Sunday School enlargement proposals prepared for congregational consideration and adoption. Organizing for Sunday School growth is more than a mechanical realignment. It is in truth a spiritual conquest.

6

PROVIDING SPACE AND EQUIPMENT
for Enlargement

A church will never grow to need the space it fails to provide. A number of years ago, this caption appeared in bold type across the middle of a blank page in the Sunday bulletin of the First Baptist Church of West Monroe, Louisiana. Since the date of this bulletin, that church has been in what might be called a continuous program of planning and constructing buildings. The sequel to each building project has been growth in the organizations. The people came in to fill them.

Similar factors are evident in a study of the twelve largest churches, from a numerical standpoint, in the Southern Baptist Convention. Almost without exception, the greatest periods of growth, as evidenced in their records, can be pinpointed within the time span involved in projecting, planning, and constructing additional space. Considerable increases were noticeable in the following areas: (1) Sunday School enrolment, (2) Sunday School attendance, (3) baptisms, (4) financial contributions, and (5) gifts to missions.

I. Recognizing the Importance of Space and Equipment

Many churches have recognized the relationship between the right kind of space and church program needs. Consequently, they have attempted to determine program needs prior to planning their buildings.

Experience has shown that a church program somehow takes the shape of the building like water assumes the shape of its container. A realization of this fact makes it highly desirable to analyze program needs well in advance of drawing plans for the building. Also, let it be noted that a building project in the majority of churches is a once-in-a-lifetime affair; and decisions regarding the arrangement of space in the building will influence for a long time what that church can do in organization.

For fear some may feel that the emphasis on physical structure is being overdone, let us note three factors usually in evidence when a church experiences phenomenal numerical growth in its church program: (1) There is a reasonable number of unenlisted prospects in the community. (2) There is a recognition of the relationship between the church program and properly arranged floor space in the building. (3) There also is an effective plan for enlisting and training the organizational leadership.

II. Conducting a Critical Church Space Survey

A recognition of the proper relationship between a church program and the building space it occupies leads us to see that the church building becomes the space vehicle in which a large part of the organized church program moves. It seems practical for a church to call for "a hold in the countdown," during which time it can make an exhaustive methodical check on the worthiness of its vehicle (building space).

1. *Surveying Available Space*

Before a congregation attempts to plan new construction, a thorough analysis of existing physical resources should be made to see where to focus attention to best meet needs. The instrument for such a survey or analysis can be found in materials provided by the Church Architecture Department at the Sunday School Board of the Southern Baptist Convention.

(1) *A space walk.*—Such a survey should begin with the pastor, minister of education, Sunday School director, or chairman of the church building survey and planning committee arranging for selected church leaders to tour the building. The best time for such a space walk would be during the Sunday School hour, so that actual conditions can be seen in the peak use period of the building. Notes of space available and crowded conditions should be made for future review and analysis.

After several such walks with selected groups, a meeting should be held to review and evaluate the findings. The results should be categorized into two lists: immediate needs and possibilities for early implementation, and long-range needs for future study by a special survey and planning committee.

(2) *In the church building.*—After completing the space walk, it is often possible to make some reassignment of space to increase the efficiency of total building usage. In a few instances such reassignments have eliminated or postponed the need for new structures.

(3) *Near the church building.*—Many times immediate needs can be met by utilizing space in other buildings near the church, such as residences, trailers, and some business establishments. Often property adjacent to the present church building is needed for future planning. It should be acquired and temporary use made of the buildings while plans are being prepared for the new structures. In rare cases such buildings may be remodeled and incorporated into the total permanent plan.

Theaters and nearby school buildings can sometimes be rented for temporary use. The church that faces a serious shortage of space should explore all possibilities in providing space for temporary, but immediate, use. A simple caution should be given against excessive expenditures on remodeling temporary structures. Seek more space, but move prudently.

2. Adjusting the Use of Space

The survey and analysis of existing space should indicate where possible reassignment or simple remodeling can make the use of all areas more efficient. An "Organization and Space Worksheet" may be found in *Preparing to Reach People* (available at Baptist Book Stores). At least once a year, the use of all building areas should be reviewed and necessary changes made. No group should be allowed to assume an attitude of permanent possession of the area it occupies.

3. Adapting the Use of Space

"Multiple use" is a term frequently employed by folding-door salesmen to promote their sales. Although there are instances in which careful planning can provide for practical use of the same area by more than one program organization, these may be kept to a minimum.

A factor in making an area serve more than one use is the provision of ample storage space. For example, individual closets or cabinets can be provided for each organization, thereby allowing Sunday School, Training Union, choral groups, and others to use the area. Careful programing can result in using certain portions of a building over and over during the week.

In first units it is sometimes desirable to utilize such multiple-use areas as an interim auditorium. In this type of approach the first unit should be designed as an educational unit in an overall plan which allows for the permanent auditorium to be constructed at a later date in the most prominent place on the site. Many churches have emphasized providing such buildings in the establishment of new work.

III. Planning for New Space

1. A Survey and Planning Committee

Building needs of a long-range nature should be handled through the survey and planning committee. Ample time should be allowed for this committee to do a thorough job, beginning with a comprehensive analysis of the total church program, both present and future.

The survey and planning committee will be relatively large, since every facet of the total church program will need to be represented on it. The church council sometimes becomes the nucleus of this committee with other persons added to provide full representation of the church program and to allow for adequate personnel on the many subcommittees.

The survey and planning committee should be instructed to (1) study church programs and organization projection; (2) determine space and equipment needs as related to these programs and organizations; (3) propose long-range plans toward providing adequate property and the necessary number of building units to carry out the programs. A *Church Property/Building Guidebook* (available at Baptist Book Stores) should be used by this committee during its period of analysis and planning.

2. A Church Building Committee

When the survey and planning committee has presented the results of its study of program needs and floor space requirements and its report has been accepted by the church as its working guide, the committee should be dismissed. The building committee is responsible for the implementation of the recommendations from the survey and planning committee as received and approved by the church. The building committee will no doubt include selected persons who served on the survey and planning committee. Persons who are familiar with such matters as building materials, construction, finances, and legal procedures should be added. The *Church Property/Building Guidebook* should be followed by that committee throughout its deliberations.

One of the first tasks of the building committee will be to select and recommend the employment of an architect. Several months will be required for the development of complete plans and specifications to be followed in the construction of the building.

3. Consultation

Throughout the tenure of service of these two committees, much can be gained by using the many sources of consultation. The Church Architecture Department of the Sunday School Board has a staff of consultants and technicians whose counsel may be had for the asking. The architectural consultants can actually visit the local churches and meet with committees on the site, if the invitations are received with ample time allowed for scheduling such conferences.

Committees and architects are welcome to visit the Nashville studios of the Church Architecture Department for conferences. Correspondence and telephone conversations can do much to help move a project along.

After meetings with the representatives of the Church Architecture Department, on the site or in Nashville, it is usually desirable for the department's technical staff of architects, engineers, and draftsmen to develop schematic plot plans and floor-plan sketches which reflect the recommendations.

After the architect has been selected, the Church Architecture Department will provide him a copy of *Church Architectural Data Sheets*. This is a manual of technical material to assist in the proper design of building space to meet the unique requirements of a Baptist church's program. Another service to the architect is that of reviewing his plans at the various design stages.

Another important resource person can be the state convention church building consultant. Every state convention organization has within its staff a person designated to serve in this capacity. He is available for consultation.

The counsel of these denominational representatives can often help a church save thousands of dollars, as well as assure the church that it is providing a structure which meets current program and organizational needs. The consultants can help a church to identify problems and mistakes which can be avoided with proper forethought and planning. It is easy to change a wall while it is a simple line on paper, but often impossible after it has taken shape in concrete, mortar, and steel.

IV. Furnishings and Equipment Needs

Often a congregation overlooks the need for including the item of furnishings and equipment in its building budget. This can prove to be quite a large amount and should be anticipated early in the program. It is not unusual for the cost of furnishings to increase the total cost of the project by as much as 15 percent.

Cost is not the only factor to consider in furnishing and equipping a building. A basic threefold test should be applied to every furnishing item: (1) Is it comfortable? (2) Is it appealing to the eye? (3) Is it durable?

1. *Furnishings Should Be Graded*

Characteristics of the people who will use the various areas of the building should be considered when specifications are developed for the purchase of furnishings. Sizes and heights for chairs and tables vary from one age group to another. The proper selection of these items depends upon a careful study of the needs of the various groups for which the church provides space and equipment. Specifications for equipment for these various groups will be found in literature presenting the department organizational needs and in materials provided by the Church Architecture Department. Special needs of handicapped or retarded people also should be considered in planning the area and furnishings they will use.

2. *Furnishings Should Be Ordered in Time*

Several months will be required for some special equipment items to be custom made. All factors should be decided early enough for items to be delivered at the time they are needed. It is often desirable to specify in the sales contract that equipment and furnishings are to be installed, rather than allow them to be unloaded and left for the custodians to unwrap and put in place.

3. *Establish Specifications*

In order to compare prices and insure meeting each department's needs, it is wise to develop a specification list which supplier's can use in working up the cost estimates they submit as a bid. One pastor suggested that the manufacturer getting the contract should be instructed to leave his samples used in securing the contract in order that the actual shipment of furniture could be compared with the sample.

Many churches would do well to pay the slight cost difference between the cheapest line of furnishings and the best. If finances are limited, it is usually desirable to order less so as to get quality materials, and to delay purchasing some items until later when the best quality can be afforded. The slight increase in cost and the temporary delay will be well repaid in the long run through many years of enjoying materials of better quality.

When purchasing pianos for departments, it is advisable to select a studio-size rather than the smallest spinet models.

V. Counting the Cost

Early in the planning of a building it is wise to determine an approximate cost for the total project. To be exact is difficult, but a good estimate will help to establish some guidelines.

An investigation into what neighbor churches have paid in recent building projects will furnish usable information. Distinction should be made between construction costs for an auditorium and those for educational units. As a general rule, auditorium costs will average about twice that of educational space on a square-footage basis. One of the most reliable sources for "rule-of-thumb" estimates is to determine the cost of constructing classroom units of public schools in any given area. This figure is usually comparable to that of church educational units.

1. *The Building Budget*

More items are required to make up the building budget than one might realize at the outset. All of them should be studied thoroughly by those in the church who are responsible for financial matters. The total amount of money available for the project must cover all items requiring expenditures during the entire program. Before the architect develops plans, it is desirable for him to receive some indication from the church regarding the financial potential for the building portion of the project.

The following items are suggestive of the total scope to be considered in arriving at an adequate building budget.

- The first item will be the cost of the building itself. In arriving at this figure there will need to be estimates of the architect's fee, land surveys and tests, special consultants' fees (such as acoustical and design), insurance, bond costs, and legal fees.
- Another item will be the cost of financing, sometimes referred to as brokerage or handling costs.
- The cost of furnishings must be included.
- Other items are usually cared for by allowing a contingency amount in the budget varying from 3 to 6 percent of the total anticipated cost.
- The cost of increased occupancy expense, such as utilities and custodial care, should be estimated and included in the regular budget estimates which will be in effect during the year the structure is entered.

2. The Building Fund

True, some churches borrow the total amount of money needed for a building program. However, the wisest approach seems to indicate the desirability of accumulating some funds before thinking about the amount to be borrowed. Usually churches with 20 to 30 percent of the project cost on hand before construction have no difficulty in arranging to borrow the balance.

A building fund can be created out of planned budget receipts, special building fund days, and appeals.

One special manner becoming popular at this writing is the "Together We Build" fund-raising campaign as outlined by the Stewardship Commission of the Southern Baptist Convention.

This campaign combines methods found in the professional fund-raising programs and many techniques found in the Southern Baptist Convention's Forward Program emphasis: Trained consultants are available to direct such campaigns. The Stewardship Commission should be contacted for further information.

3. Borrowed Funds

Banks continue to be a source for a major portion of church building program loans. This does not necessarily mean a bank loan is the best manner of building finance, for there are numerous other means available. Each case must be evaluated and the decision made on the merits of the individual requirements. No one plan is the best solution for all cases.

Some churches will find it desirable to consider issuing bonds as the means of securing building funds. Numerous bonding companies provide the service of arranging the issue and selling the bonds. Other churches may find it desirable to secure funds from such organizations as savings and loan companies or insurance companies who participate in church building loans.

Regardless of the manner of financing selected, it will be advisable to follow the guideline of limiting the total amount borrowed to a figure which calls for payments not to exceed more than the equivalent of one week's total church offering per month.

7

ENLISTING AND TRAINING WORKERS
for Enlargement

ENLISTING Sunday School workers is one of the most important actions that a church will take. This is true because of the significant role of the Sunday School in a total church program. The task of leading in the study of the Bible is of such importance as to demand the best qualities available in members of a church. The most effective work will be done and many problems solved in advance when the right persons are chosen to work in the Bible teaching program.

I. Determine Basic Qualifications for Workers

A church needs to determine and state clearly the basic qualifications desired in workers. Such action will improve the quality of work in the church, and also will help members to see the need for further development of their spiritual lives.

Obviously, some group or committee will need to make a study and propose to the church these basic qualifications. This group could be the church council or the nominating committee. In either case, it would be wise to have the assignment come from the church, with a report back to the congregation for official action. When such action is completed, a nominating committee can proceed with a clear purpose to enlist workers. They can stress the high standards which the church is encouraging.

The group which has the responsibility for proposing the desired basic qualifications could do no better than to begin with a look at God's Word as the foundation for such action. Help in determining desired qualities of church leaders is found in the Bible.

> This is a true saying: If a man is eager to be a church leader, he desires an excellent work. A church leader must be a man without fault; he must have only one wife, be sober, self-controlled, and orderly; he must welcome strangers in his home; he must be able to teach; he must not be a drunkard or a violent man, but gentle and peaceful; he must not love money; he must be able to manage his own family well, and make his children obey him with all respect. For if a man does not know how to manage his own family, how can he take care of the church of God? He must not be a man who has been recently converted; else he will swell up with pride and be condemned, as the Devil was. He should be a man who is respected by the people outside the church, so that he will not be disgraced and fall into the Devil's trap.
>
> Church helpers must also be of good character and sincere; they must not drink too much wine or be greedy; they should hold to the revealed truth of the faith with a clear conscience. They should be tested first, and then, if they pass the test, they should serve. Their wives also must be of good character, and not gossip; they must be sober and honest in everything. A church helper must have only one wife, and be able to manage his children and family well. Those who do a good work win for themselves a good standing and are able to speak boldly about the fact that is ours in union with Christ Jesus (1 Tim. 3:1–13, TEV).

In determining basic qualifications, the church will want to set the standards as high as possible and constantly try to raise them as the workers develop toward spiritual maturity. This action will encourage workers to engage in a program of personal spiritual development. For best results, the basic qualifications should be shared in printed form with the prospective worker.

Some churches may prefer to use a Sunday School worker's covenant. Such a covenant might read as follows:

SUNDAY SCHOOL WORKER'S COVENANT

Believing that the privilege of helping people seek to walk in the Christian way of life is worthy of my best, I covenant, as a worker in the Bible teaching program of my church, to—

* Order my conduct in keeping with the teachings and spirit of the New Testament, and seek the help of the Holy Spirit that I may be faithful and effective in my work (Eph. 4:1).
* Be regular and punctual in attendance; and, in case of unavoidable absence, give notice thereof as far in advance as possible (1 Cor. 4:2).
* Make thorough preparation for leading Bible study and/or for my other duties each week (2 Tim. 2:15).
* Use the Bible with my group on Sunday morning, or in other meetings, and help them to understand and love it (Ps. 119:16).
* Contribute my tithe to my church's budget (Mal. 3:10).
* Participate thoughtfully in the regular planning meetings (Luke 14:28–30).
* Visit prospects frequently and make a special effort to contact absentees each week (Matt. 18:12).
* Study one or more books from the New Church Study Course each year (Prov. 15:14*a*).
* Cooperate appropriately in the total educational plans and activities of my church (1 Cor. 3:9).
* Be loyal to my church as it seeks to be true to me, striving to attend all worship services (Heb. 10:25).
* Make witnessing a major endeavor (Luke 19:10).
* Seek to discover and help meet the needs of those with whom I come into contact, especially fellow church members and prospects for my church (Gal. 6:2).
* Pray regularly for my church, the Sunday School ministry, the officers and teachers, the Sunday School members, and the homes from which they come (1 Thess. 5:17).
* Apply the teachings of Christ in moral and social issues of my everyday life (Jas. 1:21–22).

With the help of God, I will do my utmost to keep this covenant.

Signed ———————————————— Date ————————————————

II. Enlist Sunday School Workers

Enlisting Sunday School workers is a task that must be undergirded by prayer and conducted in a spirit of positive, aggressive expectancy. Persons charged with this responsibility should face it with the assurance that when God has led in establishing a place of service he has a person to serve. Search for names—believing. Go to enlist—believing. The workers are there—find them and use them to the glory of God.

Experience in enlargement campaigns has proved that the organization can be enlarged and staffed in one week when the proper preparation and approach are made in enlisting workers. The following suggestions are made to help a church enlist workers during a campaign or at any other time that workers are needed.

1. Pinpoint the Vacancies

Determine the positions which need to be filled. Working from the chart included in chapter 3 (see p. 27), prepare a list of the vacancies. Use forms such as the ones shown on pages 83–84.

2. Prepare to Discover Potential Workers

Schedule a meeting of a small group of persons in the church who know the qualifications and abilities of the individual members. A church nominating committee which serves all year should be able to meet this need. Since the church training program usually is responsible for discovering and training potential leaders, a church may wish to include the Training Union director in this group. He could have information on persons who have completed the course on potential leader training.

3. Gather Materials

Arrange for the necessary materials to conduct the meeting. These include a church roll to identify all church members who are potential workers; lists of vacancies to be filled; and a list of prospective workers, including the names of persons who have completed the church's training for potential workers.

WORKERS NEEDED

PRESCHOOL DIVISION*

Department I (B–1)
 Director _____
 Workers _____

Department II (2–3)
 Director _____
 Workers _____

Department III (4–5)
 Director _____
 Workers _____

CHILDREN'S DIVISION**

Department I (6–7)
 Director _____
 Workers _____

Department II (8–9)
 Director _____
 Workers _____

Department III (10–11)
 Director _____
 Workers _____

YOUTH DIVISION

Department I (12–14)
 Director _____
 Teachers _____

Department II (15–17)
 Director _____
 Teachers _____

ADULT DIVISION

Department I (Single)
 Director _____
 Teachers _____
 Outreach Leaders _____

Department II (Marriage–29)
 Director _____
 Teachers _____
 Outreach Leaders _____

Department III (30–49)
 Director _____
 Teachers _____
 Outreach Leaders _____

Department IV (50–up)
 Director _____
 Teachers _____
 Outreach Leaders _____

Department V (Weektime)
 Director _____
 Teachers _____

Department VI (Adults Away)
 Director _____
 Correspondents _____

 *Cradle Roll workers also may be needed.
 **Special Education workers also may be needed.

GENERAL OFFICERS
 Director _____
 Outreach director _____
 Teaching Improvement
  director _____
 Extension director _____
 Others _____

EXTENSION ACTIVITIES
 Fellowship Bible
  class teachers _____

 Vacation Bible School
  Director _____

 Others _____

4. Conduct the Meeting

The first and most important action in the meeting is to pray for the wisdom and leadership of the Holy Spirit as workers are sought.

Distribute copies of the "workers needed" list and the "prospective workers" sheets (see illustration).

Using the church roll, look at the name of every member of the church who is a potential worker. When considering each person, ask *two* and only *two* questions: (1) Could the person serve somewhere in the Bible teaching program if he would? (2) Would this person be *acceptable to the church* according to the standards set up for workers? If the answer is negative to *either* question, consider the next person.

If the answer is affirmative to both questions, then write the

PROSPECTIVE WORKERS			
Name	Address	Telephone Number	Where Worker Could Serve Best

name, address, and *telephone number* of this person on the "Prospective Workers" list. Then indicate *where* (which department) and *what* the work is that he could do most acceptably—such as director, teacher, outreach director, outreach leader. Go through the entire church membership file in this manner.

Now consider both lists, "workers needed" and "prospective workers." Select names from the "prospective workers" list to fill in the needs as indicated on the "workers needed" list. Selecting only *one* name for each position is very important. Select department directors first, then teachers, then others. When writing names on the "workers needed" list, be sure to write in *address* and *telephone number* at the same time.

5. *Plan the Contacts*

Determine the proper person or persons to contact the prospective worker. This decision would vary according to the situation. If the nominating committee functions throughout the year, its members could serve effectively during enlargement efforts. The church may wish to use the nominating committee as a clearing-house, having the pastor, minister of education, Sunday School director, the department director, or a combination of these make the contact.

The person or persons designated to make the contact will want to hold a personal interview. Usually this would be the person with whom the prospective worker would serve. This should be arranged by an appointment in the home or at the church. Much better results are achieved when the person-to-person approach is used rather than trying to enlist workers over the telephone. The personal approach establishes better communication. It also provides an opportunity to show the prospective worker certain materials which will help him in making a decision.

Let us assume that we wish to contact a teacher for a class of adult men. Such materials as the following would be helpful: a list of the members of the class (if the class is already organized), a copy of the teacher's quarterly, and a class member's quarterly. Make arrangements to secure appropriate materials for each person to be contacted. Such planning also gives evidence to the prospective worker that the work is important.

6. *Make the Contact*

Early in the meeting tell the prospective worker why you requested the appointment. Tell him where in the organization he is needed. Emphasize the possibilities of the position, helping him to see the opportunities for serving God and his fellowman. The appeal for service should be grounded in the concept of a Christian's responsibility, with the idea of discovering the best place for each person to serve.

Show the prospective worker the helps which are available to guide him and the specific materials he would use in the new work. Share information concerning training opportunities planned in the church, association, and state, and at the two nationwide conference centers, Ridgecrest and Glorieta.

Explain that additional helps are available in the church library (if the church has one). Assure the prospective worker of the personal help and counsel of the appropriate persons in leadership positions in the organization.

Describe his duties in detail. If the church has determined basic requirements of its workers, these should be shared at this time. A copy of the "Sunday School Worker's Covenant" could be made and given to the prospective worker. Review it during the visit.

If the foregoing steps are followed, the worker can see the total picture: the opportunity, the available helps, and the total requirements of the position. Many possible future problems can be avoided by using the right approaches in enlisting persons for service in the church.

Pray with the prospective worker concerning the decision. (If he wishes more time to think and to pray about it, grant the request; but set a time by which a decision is desired. Go back to see him in person.) If he accepts the position, give him the materials which were shown earlier.

Should the prospective worker decline the opportunity, seek to determine the reason, and attempt to find the area of service in the church where his talents could best be used. (Such information could be shared with the nominating committee or with the church training program leaders, who have responsibility for leading in the discovery of potential leaders.) Before leaving, give encouragement and commendation, expressing appreciation for the opportunity of talking with the person about the church, its needs, and opportunities.

III. Plan to Train Sunday School Workers

The least a church can do for its workers is to provide opportunities for training. The church needs to recognize the value of spending time in year-round training. The task of training Sunday School workers is a permanent job because new workers are added from time to time and because all Sunday School workers need continual training.

1. The Leaders Responsible for Sunday School Training

Persons are needed in every Sunday School to work regularly at the job of training workers. The Sunday School director is primarily responsible for this task's being done well. He leads in determining training needs and in planning and directing training activities. He cooperates, of course, with his colleague in the church training program as he plans.

Other Sunday School leaders also assist in training. The assistant Sunday School director helps in every way possible. The extension director works with the teaching improvement director in improving extension activity teaching. The teaching improvement director provides all training related to the improvement of teaching. The outreach director provides, in cooperation with the church training program, Sunday School training related to outreach activities. The secretary maintains effective files related to worker training.

2. Types of Training

Sunday School workers need training both in general areas, such as Bible and Baptist doctrine, and in specific areas related to their jobs, such as administration and teaching. Courses in both areas are offered in the Church Study Course. Ideally, new workers should engage in such study before they begin to serve.

A church also needs to provide in-service training. This is not only for new workers, but for other workers who need improvement in specific areas. "The Church Study Course Catalog" provides a list of books which carry the content aids for actually training the workers. State Sunday School secretaries can provide this catalog as well as a free leaflet outlining the requirements for the Sunday School Leadership Diploma.

In order for Sunday School workers to get the training they need, numerous training opportunities should be scheduled during the year. Consider these suggestions:

- *Week of study:* four or five nights within a week
- *Two nights per week:* Monday and Thursday or Tuesday and Friday, of a two-week period
- *One night per week:* four or five weeks with one session each week
- *Friday night and all-day Saturday retreats:* four sessions on a weekend
- *Sunday afternoon:* five Sundays before Training Union, beginning midafternoon
- *Sunday evening:* coordinated with the Training Union schedule over a five- to ten-week period
- *Wednesday night:* simultaneously with the weekly planning meeting of Sunday School officers and teachers
- *Individual studies:* referred to as "home study"
- *Write-up session:* when several people who have read the same book gather for a summation session and a write-up of the book
- *Luncheon studies:* at noon, one or two days per week at a location convenient for business people
- *Dinner studies:* featuring a dinner (or supper) session one night per week for four or five weeks
- *Neighborhood studies:* morning, afternoon, or evening at a private home (living room, recreation room, patio, backyard), one session per week

Class officers need to be trained immediately after election. This task also is the responsibility of the Sunday School teaching improvement director, working with department directors. A well-trained corps of class officers can become a mighty army for action. A one-night class officers' clinic should be conducted shortly after the classes are organized and officers elected.

Many training opportunities exist outside the church. These include associational meetings, associational training schools, state Sunday School conventions and conferences, and the two nationwide conference centers, Ridgecrest and Glorieta. Local Sunday School leaders could increase the training received by their workers by encouraging attendance at such meetings. The inclusion of these assemblies in the church budget would encourage more workers to attend.

A commitment by Sunday School leaders to train their workers can produce lasting benefits to a church.

8

GOING AFTER PEOPLE—
THE PURPOSE
of Enlargement

IN THE THINKING of most Baptist church leaders through the years, "going after people" has meant "go-bring." A philosophy that is beginning to infiltrate the minds of Baptists is "go—teach." This is not a new idea, for Christ clearly indicated to his disciples: "Go ye therefore, and teach." Wherever the people are, the Bible teaching program must go.

A church does not have to make the decision of whether to "gather the people together . . . that they may hear, and that they may learn" or to "go . . . and teach." The clear implication of the Scriptures is that a church must gather people *and* go to the people.

The needs of people provide the motivation for enlargement— people who are lost, people who are not affiliated with any church, people who are unenlisted for Christ, people anywhere, and people everywhere. **Until a church recognizes the spiritual needs of persons and seeks to develop a concern that compels the members to "go," people will neither be "gathered together" nor taught where they are.**

I. Developing Christian Concern

Jesus said: "O Jerusalem, Jerusalem . . . how often would I have gathered thy children together, even as a hen gathereth her chickens under her wings, and ye would not!" (Matt. 23:37). He also said, "Let us go into the next towns, that I may preach there also: for therefore came I forth" (Mark 1:38). "When he saw the multitudes, he was moved with compassion on them" (Matt. 9:36); and he directed his disciples to go proclaiming, teaching, and ministering.

Wherever there were people, Christ expressed concern for them. Concern is a necessary first step in going after people, whether one seeks to enlist persons by Bible study or to witness to lost persons. Activity without concern reaps little harvest.

1. *The Pastor and the Deacons*

The spiritual temperature of a congregation is largely determined by its leaders. Any pastor and deacons who are content to be "thermometers" to *measure* the spiritual temperature of the congregation have not correctly ascertained nor assumed their role as church leaders. Instead, they must see themselves as "thermostats" that *determine* the spiritual temperature. A church will seldom rise above the degree of spiritual concern expressed by her leaders.

The pastor is to be the leader of the church. The attitude of following his leadership should begin with the deacons. They should be examples of the concern of Christ for the lost. The position of deacon is not to be a position of honor for honor's sake, but rather a place of service, dedication, and concern.

2. *The Church Council*

A church calendar gives a clue to a church's concern for going after people. A calendar crowded with events of minor importance that are unrelated to, and even conflict with, major outreach thrusts, symbolizes lack of focus in the concern of the church council. The responsibility of the council is to coordinate the activities suggested by the leaders of the program organizations and to establish priorities. The council should schedule the ongoing outreach activities and protect the calendar time assigned to these activities from conflicting events of lesser importance.

Members of the council should join forces with the pastor, deacons, and the Sunday School director in a concern for and a dedication to reach unsaved and unenlisted persons for Bible study and discipleship.

"Man's plight is desperate. There must be an outreach for the unreached! *There is reason for urgency in the work of the church!*" [1]

3. *The Sunday School Officers and Teachers*

The weight of the responsibility to lead in going after people falls on the Sunday School officers and teachers. They must know who the prospects are. They must develop a continuing concern for the prospects of the age group with whom they work. They must share this concern with those whom they lead. They must express this concern through establishing, maintaining, and developing a relationship with each prospect. They must provide opportunities for members to activate their concern for and interest in prospects—especially those for their age group.

In the Bible teaching program of the 70's, the outreach director has specific responsibilities to keep before the Sunday School the need for outreach to the outsider. He is responsible for maintaining an up-to-date prospect file. He will assist department outreach leaders in making assignments to responsible persons. He will assist in creating an atmosphere that will lead to witnessing and ministering actions. He will evaluate the efforts put forth to reach persons for Christ and church membership. He will counsel with the Sunday School director in approaches that need to be taken to improve the Sunday School's outreach.

4. *The Sunday School Members*

Members will seldom move out to reach people except under the guidance of effective leaders. While some Sunday School members will visit out of compassion for lost and unenlisted persons, others show little concern. They must be helped to develop motivation, and be guided.

Members may get the impression that the church staff or the officers and teachers are elected to do the work of the church. "Evangelism is not a professional job of a few gifted or trained men but is, instead, the unrelenting responsibility of every person who belongs, even in a modest way, to the Company of Jesus." [2] This is true not only of evangelism but also of Sunday School enlistment.

II. Developing Christian Witnesses

Conversion calls man to be a witness. One task that the church seeks to perform through the Bible teaching program is to lead all church members to witness daily. While the Training Union assumes the responsibility for training witnesses, the Sunday School is ideally suited to develop witnesses through actual participation in witnessing activities.

1. *The Life of the Witness*

"The primary task of the church is to witness. An important part of this witness will be given in and through the church. But the doctrine of the priesthood of all believers indicates that the major witness is to be given by Christians *in the world*." [3]

The life of an officer or teacher is a continual witness. It becomes a confusing witness when that leader says one thing and follows a different course in everyday life. "The spoken word is never really effective unless it is backed up by a life, but it is also true that the living deed is never adequate without the support which the spoken word can provide." [4]

"Yea, a man may say, Thou hast faith, and I have works: shew me thy faith without thy works, and I will shew thee my faith by my works" (James 2:18). To be really effective in verbal witnessing, a Christian life must give foundation to the witness. All that a Christian is and that he is prayerfully trying to be, the totality of his life, must be his witness to God.

2. The Skill of the Witness

The word "skill" has to do with proficiency or an acquired ability. The reference here is in relationship to "planned" witnessing efforts. While the Christian's most effective witness may be in some unplanned opportunity, or in the life he lives, he also should make opportunities for planned witnessing. This portion of the chapter will deal primarily with developing skill for such planned witnessing opportunities—opportunities which in many cases must be created.

Skilled witnessing involves: (1) the ability to share one's own testimony of salvation, telling what God has done for him through Christ; (2) an understanding and skilful handling of the Scriptures that relate to man's condition as a sinner and God's provision for man through Christ; (3) an empathy for the individual to whom witness is being given, putting oneself into another's shoes or seeing through his eyes; (4) the ability to lead an individual to confess his unworthiness before God and seek salvation in Christ; (5) the necessity of joining heart to heart with the individual and presenting him as a seeker sinner before the Savior; (6) the ability to rejoice and follow through to lead a newborn babe to "desire the sincere milk of the word, that ye [he] may grow thereby" (1 Peter 2:2).

A church is not fair to the members unless teaching and training for witnessing are provided. In most churches, the church training program assumes responsibility for training church members to witness. Sunday School leaders can work with Training Union leaders in planning such training and can encourage all Sunday School members to participate. Both classroom and clinical training seem to be necessary. Classroom training may include role-playing demonstrations, panel discussions, testimonies, questions, and answers relating to handling the hard cases, and other learning activities. However, there seems to be no substitute for assigning a "skilled" witness to each apprentice and letting the beginning witness learn from observation and experience.

3. A Plan for Development

A number of outreach plans are available from a variety of sources. However, plans for developing the one who witnesses are more limited. The Sunday School pattern of delegated responsibility and guided visitation will give developmental opportunities for witnessing, at least from an organizational standpoint. The chief concern of the Sunday School would be the leading of members to have such a relationship with Christ and with people that they recognize and take advantage of daily witnessing opportunities. (For instance—witnessing to service station attendants, waiters, or clerks.) Teachers should continually build up the faith and concern of each member so that witnessing becomes a natural process.

Love is the first requisite for daily witnessing. "Love avoids the impersonal approach and does not require a religious vocabulary (even though it be fortified with memory verses). There is no substitute for a quiet, friendly, personal talk, away from the eyes and ears of others." [5]

"Love does not substitute methods for a living relationship. Love is sensitive and seeks to discern where the Spirit is already at work in another. Love does not go off on a tangent of its own." [6]

This kind of love comes only through a right relationship with Jesus Christ. What opportunities await Sunday School leaders who can assist in developing the lives of members to be concerned, loving witnesses for Jesus Christ!

Rosalind Rinker also points out five other things that will help develop confidence in approaching a person to witness to him. Churches need to help members to be aware of and to practice these things: (1) Have a sincere regard for the individual as a person. (2) Make the atmosphere friendly and relaxed. (3) Seek to speak to the listener's need. (4) By daily preparation, be ready to have Jesus Christ walk right into the conversation. (5) Seek God's guidance in determining where the Holy Spirit is already at work in the person's life.

The new "Reaching" series of books, published by Convention Press in 1979, provides valuable help for Sunday School workers in planning a program of outreach. The titles are *Reaching People Through the Sunday School, Reaching Adults Through the Sunday School, Reaching Youth Through the Sunday School, Reaching Children Through the Sunday School*, and *Reaching Preschoolers*. Many churches have used these books with great profit. The number of concerned, dedicated witnesses has grown, the number of persons reached has increased, and the Bible teaching program has been strengthened.

At the heart of outreach are prospect study and assignment meetings. These meetings are held on age-group levels where possible, and include the workers most closely associated with the person who needs to receive the witness. Attempt is made at this meeting to consider each prospect, reviewing every effort that has been made to know him, and then to determine who should make the next contact with him. Assignments are made following this discussion.

The Program Help Series, available from the Materials Services Department, Sunday School Board, has help for a Sunday School in providing a good witnessing program. *Leading Adults to Witness* presents the need for witnessing, gives some ways to lead adults to witness, and tells how to deal with the problem of motivation. *Youth Are Witnesses, Too!* gives help in involving youth in the church's outreach program.

III. Organizing and Conducting a Program of Enlistment

Fundamental to any program of enlistment is the necessity of assigning to someone specific responsibility for the person who is to be reached. This is the secret for successful use of the Sunday School in visitation and in witnessing.

After prospects have been identified and the needed Sunday School organization has been set up, a church must consider some basic ideas if the program of enlistment is to succeed.

1. Using a Prospect File

Establishing and maintaining an accurate prospect file will succeed when one responsible person is assigned to give regular attention to the job. This person may be an office secretary on the church staff, the Sunday School secretary, outreach director, or some other qualified person.

As prospects are discovered, Prospect File Card, Form 5, should be completed for each person. (See, also, p. 52.) The Prospect File Card, Form 5, should be filed by departments and classes in a 4 by 6 file.

Prospect Visitation Assignment and Report, Form 120, or Prospect Assignment Pocket and Card also should be completed on each person so that visitation assignments can be made by the outreach director or outreach leader. The visitor would make the visit and then report to the appropriate leader. When a person who has been a prospect joins the Sunday School, the Prospect File Card, Form 5, is removed from the file.

The file of one church is shown on page 64 as an example of how the file should be arranged.

The person responsible for making visitation assignments should work through the file of each class and department regularly to see that every prospect is visited as early as possible. If visitation assignments are made from the front of each class section of the file and refiled in the back of the section after the visit has been made, this rotation of assignments will assure that no prospect is overlooked.

2. Visitation to Reach

In his book *The Ministry of Visitation*, John T. Sisemore quoted J. N. Barnette as saying: "Visitation is the chief factor in Sunday School growth, the final step is actually reaching people. A Sunday School may have adequate space, properly arranged, a sufficient number of classes, excellent teaching, attractive programs, and how vitally essential they are; but the one thing without which all these will be at least a partial failure is visitation." [7] People must know they are wanted.

A continuous, systematic visitation program is essential to the ongoing outreach activity of a church. "The desire to reach more people is more than a craze for numbers; it is a passion for souls!" [8] "The Lord's people must learn that the Lord's business must be done in the Lord's way. Visitation is the only answer to consistent Sunday School growth." [9]

Sisemore indicates that there are at least six major factors in developing a systematic program of visitation. (1) Maintain a permanent visitation program. (2) Give adequate publicity. (3) Prepare definite visitation assignments. (4) Secure adequate reports. (5) Train the visitors carefully. (6) Inspire the workers.

These factors will have to be undergirded by concern for the lost, dedicated leadership, and belief in the power of the Holy Spirit to move in the hearts of lost men and women.

3. A Plan for Prospect Visitation

The following are some essentials of a plan for visitation that is being used successfully by many churches over the Southern Bap-

---

VISITOR'S ENLISTMENT CARD

Department _____

Class _____

Name 1. _____

Name 2. _____

Check One

Thursday A.M. _____   Thursday P.M. _____

Need transportation   _____

Can furnish transportation   _____

Need nursery   _____

Suggested Form

tist Convention. This plan is built on an adequate knowledge of prospects and an accurate, up-to-date prospect file.

(1) *Know who is to visit.*—The following steps are suggested:

On Sunday mornings, include a visitor's enlistment card with the record materials for each Adult class and a card for each department in the other age groups. Each week secure two visitors from each Adult class and two visitors from each of the other departments. Insist that classes and departments return the enlistment cards with their Sunday School records Sunday morning.

Compile a list by departments and classes of those planning to visit and the time when they have agreed to visit.

On Monday, contact by form letter those outreach leaders of classes and directors of departments who did not return the Visitor's Enlistment Card. Contact on Wednesday afternoon, by telephone, any classes or departments still not reporting.

(2) *Select prospects for visitation.*—On the day before visitation day, select from front of department and class files two or three prospect cards, choosing on the basis of persons going visiting. Consider geographical location in assigning. Make visitation assignments, clipping Prospect Visitation Assignment and Report, Form 120, to the back of Visitor's Enlistment Card.

One hour before visitation time, place assignments by classes and departments on table or visitation board. Arrange meeting place.

(3) *Set definite time.*—Set at least two times to meet with visitation teams on visitation day. Start on time. Begin with prayer. Include brief planned instructions on visitation techniques. Suggest follow-up cultivation visitation of assigned prospects.

Call for special prayer requests (may be based on assignments). Spend time in specific prayer. Go out and visit. Return to church for reporting and fellowship. Leave cards with visitation results noted.

(NOTE: In large city areas, where traffic and distance may be a problem, assignments may be available on Wednesday night and cards returned the following Sunday. Other adaptations, not short-cuts, may prove to be helpful to overcome specific problems.)

(4) *Update prospect information.*—Transfer usable information from visitor's return card to permanent prospect file. Check each card carefully and refer the name to the pastor, if warranted. Refile card in back part of class or department file to insure its working through the file.

This plan is as successful as the leadership makes it. It is important to keep up with the plan weekly and to urge representation from the departments and classes.

4. A Plan for Prospect Enrollment

Many churches are now using a plan designed specifically to enroll persons in Sunday School. Persons are enrolled in the home, over the telephone, or wherever they are discovered. Under this plan, they are not required to attend before being enrolled. The only prerequisite is consent to be enrolled.

The plan was developed by E. S. Anderson, while pastor of Riverside Baptist Church, Fort Myers, Florida. The church grew from 1,094 enrolled in 1972 to 2,242 in 1974, with average attendance increasing from 440 to 913 during this period. Other churches have experienced similar results.

The plan calls for involving a large number of church members in the enrollment campaign through door-to-door visitation, telephone, youth groups enrolling youth, the bus ministry, and a pastor's Sunday School class. The pastor endeavors to enroll unenrolled church members and others among his acquaintances in this special class. These new enrollees are then transferred to existing classes and departments as soon as they are willing.

One week of enrollment is followed by four weeks of intensive follow-up, including contacts by the pastor, teachers, group leaders, and the persons originally doing the enrolling. Every effort is made to secure the attendance of the new enrollees during this time.

This plan is entitled "ACTION: A Reach Out Enrollment Plan for Sunday School." Guidance materials are available from the Sunday School Department, Sunday School Board.

For additional information, write to Growth Section, 127 Ninth Avenue, North, Nashville, Tennessee 37234, or the state Sunday School director.

5. *Visitation That Evidences Concern*

A man and his wife, workers with married young adults in a university-center church, went to call on a couple to invite them to Sunday School. The couple lived quite near the church. The visitors were shocked and sorry to hear the young man say: "People from your church have visited us several times while we have been here in school. And we have always gotten the impression that all you people want to do is increase your enrolment. Not one time has a visitor made me feel he wanted to get to know me, or that he would be concerned about me if I weren't a prospect for his class. We are about to leave the city and I just thought you should know this."

Shirley was sixteen and had not been to Sunday School since she was promoted to the Youth department. She had never made a profession of faith. As the workers in the Youth department studied the enrolment, they pondered how they might go about enlisting Shirley. They decided on a different approach. The director and the teacher went to Shirley's house and visited for a few moments. The church was not mentioned at all that time. The visits were repeated at two-week intervals. Always there were friendly conversation, questions about school, talk about the latest records, and some casual reference to youth activities at the church—still no mention of Sunday School. On the fifth visit, Shirley could stand it no longer. She said, "When are you all going to get around to telling me that I ought to be in Sunday School?" The director then explained that while they were concerned about her being in Sunday School, that was not their deepest concern. The main point, the visitors told Shirley, was to get to know her and to help her get to know the Lord. The result was that Shirley did decide to come to Sunday School; she proved helpful in preparation for many youth activities; and before the year was over she had made a profession of her faith.

Unchurched people are responding only to the kind of visitation that evidences concern in them personally. It must be the kind of visitation that can best be described as "cultivation visitation." Cultivation visitation can be encouraged and can be made meaningful through the use of a planned approach.

Cultivating the person who needs to become involved in Bible study or one who needs to know the Savior is the goal of effective visitation. To do this kind of visitation, one must first of all be concerned about the needs of a person.

6. Meaningful Involvement to Hold

There is considerable difference between "activity" and "involvement." Oftentimes a church will seek to enlist a new Christian in all of the activities of the church without leading the person to see the relevance of these activities to his new way of life or why he should participate. In so doing, he may join thousands of other busy Southern Baptists whose "busyness" has taken the place of meaningful involvement in one's commitment to Christian discipleship.

In his book *Pastoral Evangelism*, Samuel Southard indicates that each convert needs help in at least four areas of faith and life. He needs: (1) an adequate interpretation of his Christian experience, (2) recognition by Christian people who seem important, (3) opportunity for personal unburdening, and (4) instruction in Christian living.

The Sunday School and the Training Union are the organizations which meet these needs. The new church member orientation plan for Southern Baptist churches will lead new members to meaningful involvement.

"How may a Sunday School class have significance for new Christians? If the teacher lectures, it will add little more than assorted biblical information. But if there is participation through discussion, the convert will have opportunity to see how other people feel about questions of religion in life. He also can test his own ideas with a sympathetic group that is controlled by a concern for the accurate biblical witness in modern application." [10]

[1] Findley B. Edge, *A Quest for Vitality in Religion* (Nashville: Broadman Press, 1963), p. 151.

[2] Elton Trueblood, *The Company of the Committed* (New York: Harper and Row, 1961), p. 55.

[3] Edge, *op. cit.*, pp. 140–41.

[4] Trueblood, *op. cit.*, p. 53.

[5] Rosalind Rinker, *You Can Witness with Confidence* (Grand Rapids: Zondervan, 1962), p. 37.

[6] *Ibid.*

[7] John T. Sisemore, *The Ministry of Visitation* (Nashville: Convention Press, 1954), p. 65.

[8] *Ibid.*, p. 67.

[9] *Ibid.*, p. 68.

[10] Samuel Southard, *Pastoral Evangelism* (Nashville: Broadman Press, 1962), pp. 112–13.

9

BECOMING A CHURCH
THAT CAN GO

THE QUESTION often is asked: Will the church meet the challenge of this revolutionary period in history? A prior question may need to be answered: *Can* the church meet the challenge of this revolutionary period in history? Considerable evidence shows that before most churches can make significant progress in their ministering roles in the world, internal change must be achieved.

The lives of the great hosts of nonresident and inactive church members bear undeniable testimony to the validity of this statement: "Christianity has not been tried and found wanting. It has been tried and found difficult. And consequently many have ceased trying." [1]

I. Trends Which Must Be Faced

A compromised and powerless faith such as is held and practiced by many persons in thousands of churches today has never had a significant influence on the world. Many individuals who respond to it in their quest for a genuine faith later discover the shallowness of such faith and openly repudiate their earlier profession or simply drift away, giving their loyalty to other interests. Robert Raines wrote:

> In the hour of the church's institutional success, its spiritual failure is being exposed. In the 1950's hungry men and women flocked into the churches seeking new life and were often handed, instead, old programs. They discovered that they could become and remain lost just as easily in the church as in the community service club, and far more poignantly. Many nibbled at the edges of the crust but never found the bread of life. So in the 1960's we see signs of the ebb of this surging hope, as people drift out of the church, disillusioned by the discovery that the church did not deliver on its promise of new life in Christ.[2]

In the 70's Southern Baptists are seriously affected by this frightening condition. Though church membership continues to increase, the percentage of church members who are actively involved in churches' life and witness is decreasing. The number of professions of faith in relation to the total number of church members decreased from a ratio of one to twenty in 1955, to one to thirty in the late 60's. The percentage of church members who participate regularly in the church's Bible teaching program continues to decrease. Increased financial gifts in most churches result from inflationary influences and do not necessarily reflect deeper stewardship commitments. When conditions are viewed in the light of the more intangible fruit of the Spirit (see Gal. 5:22) the picture is equally disturbing.

While many churches spend most of their time maintaining their institutional structures, the world about them becomes more pagan. World population increases at the rate of approximately sixty million each year. Only one person out of six of the population increase identifies with any Christian church. Unless drastic changes take place, the Christian church as we know it today is in serious danger of being overrun by pagans both from within its own membership and from the world that surrounds it.

The undemanding type of institutional religion on which the present generation has grown up has made few demands on its adherents. It has not always called for radical separation from the world and deep personal commitment to the Lord and his hard and narrow way. The result is that many people honestly do not realize what the requirements of their professed faith really are.

If the foregoing appraisal sounds negative, let it be remembered that history records instances in which God has allowed generations to wander in spiritual wildernesses until a new generation under new leaders responded to his call to worthy worship and service.

Christ's kingdom is founded on his own personal sacrifice. It advances on the personal sacrifices of his subjects. The deeper and more significant goals of Sunday School enlargement depend entirely on the willingness of Sunday School officers and teachers to give themselves in obedience and sacrificial service. The cause of Christ calls for aggressive action. Only in this manner can the influence of the church be established.

II. Conditions Which Must Be Changed

Three conditions in many Baptist churches must be corrected before they can experience any significant advance in reaching lost people for Christ and church membership. These conditions prevail to some degree in most churches. They may be viewed as reasons for the declining influence and the slowdown in evangelistic outreach of many churches. However, a more positive view would suggest that they are a challenge and an opportunity for such expansion.

1. *Unregenerate Lives*

Why are so many people who are identified as church members not meaningfully involved in their church? No doubt there are many reasons. Many concerned pastors and laymen believe that the primary reason is lack of a new birth. It seems apparent that many of these "church members" do not know the Lord of the church and, therefore, cannot be meaningfully involved in the Lord's work.

This is a serious charge for Baptists, whose most distinguishing doctrine through the centuries has been their concept of the church. Central to this concept is the claim that only regenerate persons can be members. Despite the traditional definition of a church, how many Baptists can honestly maintain that their church is solely a "body of baptized believers"? Too much evidence points to an indication that among those whose names are on church rolls are some who are not believers.

Recently in an evangelism class in a Southern Baptist seminary, the students were asked to relate their conversion experience to the class. As the reports continued, so many of these theology students indicated that they were converted after they joined a church, that the professor polled the entire class on the matter. He learned that 60 percent of these students dated their conversion after they were received as members by some church. The professor made this significant remark: "You made a mistake but discovered the error of your way. What of the thousands who made the same mistake but still do not know it?"

According to a recent study, 7.2 percent of the Adult leaders in Southern Baptist churches have been reimmersed because they realized they were not converted when they were first baptized.[3] Again the questions may be posed: What of the thousands who have never been led to test the reality of their profession of faith? How many of the nominal church members have never had a genuine experience of grace? These are disturbing questions, but they must be faced.

The unregenerate condition of many church members must be corrected if church membership is to have integrity and meaning. There should be a concentrated effort to win the lost church members. This is a delicate matter and would at first seem to demand that concerned members become judges. This is not necessarily true. When a person does not respond to any of his church's appeals, when he evidences none of the fruits of a Christian, it is not judging to assume that person has spiritual problems; and that one of his problems may be that he is unsaved. This may mean personally confronting such persons lovingly but positively with the basic claims of the gospel. One witness is not adequate. A continuing witness must be given to anyone and everyone who does not give genuine evidence of a vital relationship with the Lord. What can be done if there are those who refuse to respond to this loving witness and continue in a life of sin and indifference? Many feel that if a church is to seek integrity in its witness, it has little choice but to sever its relationship with such members. This is a serious matter which each church must come to terms with and for which each church will choose its own course of action.

A program of ministry to lost, uncommitted, and estranged church members may be outlined from a study of Matthew 18: 1–35. For the full message of the chapter to be understood, it must be viewed as a whole. Each section builds on the preceding sections.

- Recognize the nature of true church members and begin with a biblical emphasis on the nature and necessity of the new birth (Matt. 18:1–4).
- Recognize and accept the responsibility of the church in dealing with the new and immature members (Matt. 18:5–9).
- Demonstrate the love and concern which a church should have for its members when they wander away (Matt. 18:10–14).
- Take specific and immediate steps to heal a ruptured fellowship, even to the point of discipline when a brother is unrepentant for the rupture.
- Cultivate and demonstrate Christian attitudes toward disciplined brothers.

These are church actions, and the task of leading church members to perform the functions of a church is a church task. However, a church can do much through the Bible teaching program to take the actions called for in Matthew 18.

The foundations for such actions as those suggested in Matthew 18 must be laid through the interpretation of conversion, discipleship, and church membership as it is done in teaching the biblical revelation. The responsibility for reaching and meaningfully involving members in the life of the church is carried mainly by those who work in and through the Sunday School. Likewise, each of the other actions outlined in Matthew 18 is taken by the church through the Sunday School or on foundations which are laid by the Sunday School through teaching the biblical revelation.

2. Uncommitted and Undisciplined Lives

Christian discipleship is rooted in a disciplined life. The covenant commitments of church membership make some of the loose and irresponsible attitudes toward church membership unthinkable.

> Although it is true that a majority of present-day Americans are members of some church, this does not mean that they have given themselves to God to do his will "on earth even as it is done in heaven." The fact is that the labor union, the manufacturers' association, or the professional society of which they are members exerts far more influence on their attitudes, values, and courses of action. These relationships demand and get far more real loyalty from the average man than does the church to which he belongs.
>
> Modern society expects the church to make a comfortable adjustment to current social norms, and the church usually has been ready to comply. The distinctions between church and world, between the people of God and the people of the world, has largely been lost. The masses join the churches with a minimum of commitment and with a minimum being expected of them.[4]

The Bible teaching program of a church must relate to this problem. Sunday School officers and teachers must teach, by precept and example, both the privilege and the responsibility of Christian discipleship and church membership. Christ's call to discipleship is rewarding but demanding. The gate to life is narrow, and the road is hard. Let the demand of Jesus be remembered: "'If any man would come after me, let him *deny himself* and take up his cross and follow me. For whoever would save his life will lose it, and whoever loses his life for my sake will find it'" (Matt. 16:24–25, RSV).

This level of discipleship should be reflected in the church's membership standards, in its requirements for leadership assignments, and in the general atmosphere and spirit that prevail in the church. Enlarging and improving the Bible teaching program as described in this book can be a step in that direction.

3. *Lives That Show Little Love*

The most distinguishing characteristic of a church should be its love for people, both those who are church members and those who are not. However, church members find loving difficult. It takes courage and humility.

> Love is the capacity to reveal yourself to another, and to let another reveal himself to you. It is a new kind of seeing. Love is the capacity to be reconciled to another, and to let another be reconciled to you. It is a new kind of being. God makes it possible for us to love one another because He first loved us. He has revealed Himself to us in Christ and reconciled us to Himself through Christ. We learn Christ's love by learning to love one another and thus release his gracious gifts in one another.[5]

In surveying the condition that prevails in the modern church, Robert Raines goes on to charge:

> There is in our fellowship a colorless insipidity and an absence of unique relationship. The salt has lost its savor, the light grows dim in the dark world, the leaven appears lost in the lump, and the sheep look very much like the wolves. If Jesus' question to the first disciples were put to us, ". . . . what is there extraordinary about . . . [your behavior]?" (Matt. 5:47, NEB), we would have to answer, "Nothing." If our discipleship is to be known in the world by the quality of our love for one another (John 13:35), can we wonder that to a world walking in shadowed valleys, the church does not look like a city set on a hill?[6]

Love as it is conceived in this discussion is not indulgent pampering of people as they pursue their selfish and material-oriented goals. It is actions a church takes toward becoming a committed and disciplined church to be used by God in his reconciliation ministry to the world. It is making clear the demanding requirements of discipleship so that all may understand that life comes through death, reward through sacrifice, and union with Christ through a personal transformation which makes one an alien to the world. It is caring enough to attack intentionally and openly the self-centeredness that would prevent the church from becoming expendable for its Lord. It is fulfilling covenant commitments to those who seek the benefits and opportunities of a church's fellowship.

Such love calls for cross-bearing, the death of self, and a life under the control of Jesus Christ. It denies "cheap grace"; it declares that Christ must become Lord if he is to be Savior. It sets the standards for Christian discipleship and church membership and accepts the "narrow gate and hard road" as the lot and privilege of the church. Finally, such love focuses on the necessity of a church's *being* what it is supposed to be before it can *do* what it is supposed to do.

III. Commitments Which Must Be Made

Church and kingdom advance do not wait for human resources and "know-how." Never have so many resources, of both personnel and material, been available for church work. Most churches have members who have the knowledge and skill to do the work that needs to be done. The one thing most obviously missing in our day is the will to give ourselves. Without personal dedication, other resources are worth little.

A halfhearted commitment has never been acceptable to God. It is equally unacceptable to man. Churches are being challenged to demonstrate Christian faith in actions and in relationships to people both in and out of the church.

1. *The Basic Call of Discipleship*

Christ's invitation was: "'Come to me, all who labor and are heavy laden . . . take my yoke upon you, and learn from me'" (Matt. 11:28-29, RSV). This invitation magnifies the hope and security which a person has when he follows Christ. It suggests, but does not amplify, the conditions on which this hope and security are based. Inner hope and security can be experienced in a world of turmoil and hate (Matt. 10:34-39). Christ also was careful to define the conditions necessary for one to identify with him (Luke 9:57-62; Matt. 16:24-25).

Then and now, one basic condition is required for identification with Christ: he must become Lord. Self-will must be subordinated to Christ's will. This act of surrender must be an accomplished fact without any known reservation. It must be a continuing experience in daily renewal. Finally, it must become a goal toward which a person works because, as he succeeds in making Christ Lord of his life, one becomes more conscious of how far short he falls from his spiritual goal. Not all Christians can perform at the same level and with the same degree of effectiveness. However, all should perform with the same devotion to their Lord.

2. *The Call to Holy Living*

In the born-again life, holiness and dedication are both a fact and a continuing experience. Paul's plea for dedication was addressed to persons who knew the Lord (Rom. 12:1-2). Yet, they needed to know him in a new and more transforming way day by day. This need emphasizes a dimension of Christian discipleship that is too often neglected. The essence of Paul's appeal seems to be for the Christian to let God so fill and rule in his life that at least two things happen: (1) A radical and obvious transformation is brought about by God's indwelling presence. (2) The life, thus transformed and endued with power, becomes a changing influence in the world. We are not to conform. We are to be transformed, and in so doing we will be a transforming influence for God.

3. *The Call to the Servant's Role*

Few concepts are more basic to the message of the New Testament than the concept that churches and individual Christians are servants, ministering in the name of their Lord. Christ reminded his disciples: "'Whoever would be great among you must be your servant, and whoever would be first among you must be your slave; even as the Son of man came not to be served but to serve, and to give his life a ransom for many'" (Matt. 20:26-28, RSV).

A modern version of this biblical admonition appeared in the form of a sign behind the desk at Ridgecrest Baptist Assembly a few years ago. The sign read: "It's nice to be important. It's more important to be nice." Leading churchmen from across the Southern Baptist Convention passed by this desk. Some staffer, sensing the gentle attitude of which Christ spoke, used the sign to emphasize a basic trait which should characterize churches and each individual Christian.

It is hard for an institutionalized, world-oriented church to assume the servant's role. Such a role is incompatible with the church's usual prominent place in the power structure of the community. The influence of this power structure is readily discernible. The silent penetrating influence of a committed spiritual fellowship, though discernible by all, is attractive only to spiritual-minded men or men under the convicting influence of the Spirit of God.

The servant's role requires reliance upon the resources of God. When a church relies upon the resources of God, many human resources may be withdrawn. Many others must be abandoned by a church because they are unreliable or incompatible with the goals of the church. But how can we meet the challenge of a lost world unless we lay ourselves at the feet of our Lord and say: "Command me . . . I am your servant"?

IV. Commands Which Must Be Obeyed

Churches are under divine orders. These orders are not optional. They are binding on every person who is the recipient of God's grace through Christ. The commission of Christ to his church can be summarized under four headings.

1. To Witness

The content and scope of the Christian's witness are greater than is realized by many persons who claim to be witnesses.

The life and work of Christ on earth were finished, and he was about to return to the Father. The generation of his day and the generations to come needed to know of him and his work. His disciples, empowered by the Holy Spirit, would be his witnesses. Those who responded to Christ through their witness would in turn become witnesses. To what were they to witness? They were to witness to the entire gospel. Paul summarized the gospel:

> Have this mind among yourselves, which you have in Christ Jesus, who, though he was in the form of God, did not count equality with God a thing to be grasped, but emptied himself, taking the form of a servant, being born in the likeness of men. And being found in human form he humbled himself and became obedient unto death, even death on a cross. Therefore, God has highly exalted him and bestowed on him the name which is above every name, that at the name of Jesus every knee should bow, in heaven and on earth and under the earth, and every tongue confess that Jesus Christ is Lord, to the glory of God the Father (Philippians 2:5–10, RSV).

When this statement is analyzed, something of the content and scope of the Christian's witness emerges.

- It proclaims Christ's relationship to the Father and declares that man's most basic need is to be reconciled to the Father (2 Cor. 5:17–21).
- It portrays Christ in a servant's role of loving ministry to man and presses his standard: "'As you did it to one of the least of these my brethren, you did it to me'" (Matt. 25:40, RSV).
- It shows that Christ became obedient to the Father, even unto death, and it defines the pattern and the plan by which sinners come alive to God.
- It proclaims Jesus' place of honor and authority and asserts that one day all must stand before him. "Every knee should bow . . . every tongue confess that Jesus Christ is Lord" (Phil. 2:10–11, RSV).

2. To Make Disciples

Several facts seem pertinent in this brief consideration of our Lord's command to witness.

First, discipleship is to be understood in its broad biblical dimensions. It involves a realization of personal guilt. It involves repentance and faith. It involves God's redemptive response to man's faith and repentance. It involves a new person in Christ, one who by will and design follows a new pattern of life and produces a new product in life. Discipleship which is not characterized by all of these qualities is not genuine discipleship.

Second, the method by which disciples are made is significant. A study of Jesus' approach is revealing. We have the record of his personal encounters, his teaching and preaching, and his acts of mercy. All of these were used as methods of making disciples. However, undergirding and overshadowing these methods were Jesus' life and his relationship to the Father. These so influenced what he said and did that men sought him out.

This same quality of self-giving characterized the witness of the early church. When Peter and John stood before the council in Jerusalem, that these men "had been with Jesus" (Acts 4:13) was obvious. Every effort at making disciples must be backed by a life that demonstrates what discipleship is. For this reason Jesus admonished his disciples to wait for power (Acts 1:4). This is the desperate need of the church today—an infilling of spiritual power to give sharpness, appeal, and validity to its witness. Without this, all of the methods by which we seek to make disciples are empty and ineffective.

3. *To Equip the Disciples*

Christian maturity is the goal. Between this goal and the sinner's transforming encounter with Christ is a long, hard road of growth and development. Jesus did not separate the command to make disciples and the command to teach them. He did not conceive of doing the first without the second. Neither can we.

4. *To Represent Christ in Life and Work*

Closely related to the command to witness is the command to represent Christ in the world. "'As the Father has sent me, even so send I you'" (John 20:21, RSV). Jesus was sent to represent the Father on earth. The Christian also is sent. Jesus was sent to give himself to redeem lost men. The Christian is to give himself in the same purpose. Jesus communicated this purpose through acts of love and mercy and finally in the supreme sacrifice on the cross. The cross of the Christian involves much of what Christ's cross involved—except physical death. However, let us not forget the Christian martyrs who have gone before us. Neither let us flinch at the thought of Christian martyrs in the future. This may be the price many followers of Christ in our generation will have to pay to be loyal in their commitments.

A missionary related an experience which sounds the appropriate note to end this book. He reported that when he went to the mission field his prayer was: "Lord, help me to do my work for you." As he matured, his prayer became: "Lord, help me to do your work." Finally, as he neared retirement, his prayer became, "Lord, do your work through me." Should that not be every Christian's prayer? Is not that the need of our day? Like Isaiah, let us come into the presence of God, be cleansed, and then say: "'Here I am! Send me'" (Isa. 6:8, RSV).

---

[1] H. Leo Eddleman, *Teachings of Jesus in Matthew 5–7* (Nashville: Convention Press, 1955), p. 1.

[2] Robert Raines, *Reshaping the Christian Life* (New York: Harper and Row, 1964), p. 3.

[3] Research Project—003, *Adult Leadership in Southern Baptist Churches,* Volume A, 1966, p. 61.

[4] Findley B. Edge, *A Quest for Vitality in Religion* (Nashville: Broadman Press, 1963), p. 20.

[5] Raines, *op. cit.*, p. 20.

[6] *Ibid.*, p. 2.

Personal Learning Activities

Chapter 1

1. State the threefold purpose of a Sunday School enlargement program.
2. State three truths that serve to establish a biblical basis for enlargement.
3. How does a Christian's involvement in outreach for enlargement relate to his calling as a priest?
4. What is still the soundest approach toward helping a person come to know the Lord?

Chapter 2

5. What are some benefits that a church gains from a study of enlargement needs?
6. Name the three tasks of the Sunday School that are considered in a Sunday School enlargement campaign.
7. What are the five goals of a good Sunday School program?

Chapter 3

8. Why is the correct ratio of workers to members an important factor in reaching people?
9. When may responsibility for outreach be said to be appropriately delegated?
10. Give two reasons churches should consider giving priority attention to organizing more classes and departments for adults.
11. To improve the quality of prospect visits, what specific phases may be studied?
12. Name five steps in applying Sunday School principles of growth.

Chapter 4

13. State the objective of any type of prospect search.
14. What persons constitute prospects for Bible study in a Baptist church?

15. List at least seven ways these prospects can be discovered.

Chapter 5

16. Name four essentials of an effective Sunday School organization.
17. In a church, who is responsible for initiating an enlargement of the Sunday School?
18. What factors determine how much enlargement should be attempted?
19. Why is organizing for Sunday School growth called a spiritual conquest?

Chapter 6

20. Interpret the relationship of church buildings and church program.
21. Outline the difference between the long-range committee and the building committee.
22. Name a threefold test that should be applied to every furnishing item.

Chapter 7

23. Why should a church adopt basic qualifications for its workers? What group should propose these qualifications to the church?
24. State an underlying spiritual principle of worker enlistment.
25. What procedure should be followed in contacting prospective workers after they have been selected?
26. What obligations does a church have when workers are enlisted?

Chapter 8

27. How can concern for people be developed?
28. What are the factors in developing a systematic program of visitation?

Chapter 9

29. What trends have taken place in the past decade that reflect the need of a spiritual revival in our churches?
30. What approaches can be taken to correct the unregenerate church membership problem?
31. What commitments should your church make to meet the challenge of a lost world?
32. Based on a study of this book, what personal commitments to the Lord will you make?

Teaching Suggestions

Adapted from Suggestions by Frank Voight

LISTED BELOW are some ideas which the teacher may find helpful in preparing to teach using this book. Since this book will most often be used in connection with enlargement campaigns, the following suggested schedule may be helpful.

It is suggested that chapter 1 be taught on Sunday morning to the combined Adult departments. After records and announcements, the classes may convene in the auditorium or other large assembly area. The lecture method would be your basic teaching approach, with use of Bible research and visual aids where possible.

Chapter 2 could be taught during the Training Union session on Sunday evening, once again using the large group approach with all adults together in the large assembly area.

Chapters 3 through 9 should be taught in a large assembly room,

TEACHING SCHEDULE

SUNDAY SCHOOL SESSION	"The Biblical Basis for Enlargement"
TRAINING UNION SESSION	"The Need and Goals for Enlargement"
MONDAY	"Understanding and Applying the Principles of Enlargement"
TUESDAY	"Identifying the Possibilities for Enlargement" and "Organizing for Enlargement"
WEDNESDAY	"Providing the Space and Equipment for Enlargement" and "Enlisting and Training Workers for Enlargement"
THURSDAY	"Going After People—the Purpose of Enlargement" and "Becoming a Church That Can Go"

church dining room, or auditorium. It would be best to have groups seated around tables or in a place where small groups can be formed quickly. It would be helpful to have classes and/or departments seated around table(s) together to facilitate group discussion of enlargement needs in each unit of the Sunday School.

TEACHING ENRICHMENT SUGGESTIONS

General Suggestions

- Pray for spiritual guidance and alertness.
- Make a large graph showing a growth study of the Sunday School for the past ten to twenty years.
- Create a good climate for study with room arranged according to size of group and method used, appropriate books, and good lighting.
- Have available complete information from a prospect search which included a census and a listing of church members not on the Sunday School roll. Prospect Visitation Assignment and Report, Form 120, should be completed on all prospects.
- Prepare a study of class and department enrolment and average attendance by departments and classes.
- Prepare a flip chart listing the principles of Sunday School growth as found in chapter 3.
- If desired, plan for a business meeting of the church on Wednesday to consider recommendations for enlargement and improvement of the Sunday School.
- Study thoroughly A GUIDE TO SUNDAY SCHOOL ENLARGEMENT, making notes as to illustrations and ideas that will help you to personalize the teaching of the book.
- Consider the possible use of audiovisuals. Some excellent films and filmstrips that contribute to a study of enlargement are:

Filmstrips.—*Enlarging a Sunday School,* 50 frames, color manual recording; *A Sunday School Visitation Program,* 50 frames, color, manual recording; *Outreach for Unenrolled Children,* 45 frames, color, recording. (CAVE Plan members may order these Broadman filmstrips with others from Broadman Films Department, Sunday School Board, 127 Ninth Avenue, North, Nashville, Tennessee 37234. All other customers may order these filmstrips from any Baptist Book Store.)

Film.—*Gateway to Growth,* 30 minutes, color, rental $15.00. (All Broadman motion pictures are available in Baptist Film Centers. When booking motion pictures, CAVE Plan members should specify that they are CAVE Plan members. This is necessary for proper crediting of accounts.)

Chapter 1

- Prepare a large poster outline of the book by chapter headings.
- Prepare a large poster outline of the chapters to be taught.
- Have a portable chalkboard available for all sessions.
- Display the poster with the outline of this chapter, including the four main chapter divisions.
- With a magic marker or crayon, write the number of people on the Sunday School roll across the poster outline of chapter 1. Write the number of prospects found in the prospect search and add the two. Then point out to the group that this is the basis upon which God expects you to plan this week. Read Luke 15:4–6.

Chapter 2

- Use a flip chart to outline the basic tasks of a Sunday School. Use a page for each task. Discuss each task listed. They are:
  1. Outreach
  2. Bible teaching
  3. Performance
- On the fourth page of the flip chart, write *Outreach, Bible Teaching, Performance*. Discuss their inseparability.

Chapter 3

- Multilith "A Study of Bible Teaching Possibilities" for each person in the class. Fill in appropriate blanks for each department as to number enrolled, prospects, total possibilities, total number of departments now, total number of classes now, total number workers now.
- Prepare a poster or ask a volunteer to write on the chalkboard the well-known formula for Sunday School growth advanced by Arthur Flake.
  1. Know your possibilities
  2. Enlarge the organization
  3. Provide the needed space
  4. Enlist and train the workers
  5. Go after the people

Chapter 4

- Prepare a poster or list on the chalkboard possible ways of enlargement within the walls of the church. These should include provision for weektime Bible study, new Bible study classes and departments in the Sunday School, and other possibilities.

- List the possibilities of enlargement beyond the walls of the church building. These should include Adults Away departments, fellowship Bible classes, new Sunday Schools, and other extension activities.

Chapter 5

- Place above the door of each department and each class a poster bearing the name, enrolment, prospects, total possibilities, and average attendance of each unit.
- Plan to conduct a tour of the building. A pointer of some type would be helpful for the leader of the tour. Point to the poster at each door, giving enrolment, prospects, possibilities, average attendance. Point out equipment needs as recommended by the Church Architecture Department of the Sunday School Board. *It is important that this tour be made.*
- Work up an Adult profile chart to show Adult grouping pattern.

Chapter 6

- Mimeograph a true-false test as a review.

True-False Quiz

1. A church must reach outside its walls to follow the example of Christ. (true)
2. The Bible indicates that it is possible for the cause of Christ to be lost by the unfaithfulness of a single generation of people. (true)
3. It is more difficult to get personal involvement in a large class. (true)
4. The lecture method of teaching should never be used in a Sunday School class. (false)
5. The neglect of only one principle of enlargement may hinder a Sunday School's growth. (true)
6. The best way to make new class units is to regroup the entire Sunday School or department on an age (or school) basis. (true)
7. Since children are adaptable, basement space is ideal for their departments. (false)
8. Records are only important for the registering of attendance. (false)
9. An annual promotion or advancement is essential to maintaining a well-graded Sunday School. (true)

10. The Vacation Bible School is one of the best sources of prospects for the Sunday School. (true)

Chapter 7

- Using the "Workers Needed" chart on page 83, list possible workers to fill vacancies in the enlarged organization. This should be done in a meeting with the pastor, Sunday School director, church nominating committee, and church training director. Follow the six-step procedure on pages 82–87 in working with the committees to write and contact workers. If possible, names of workers should accompany the recommended, enlarged organization structure.
- Obtain copies of "The Church Study Course Catalog" from the state Sunday School secretary.

Chapter 8

- Prepare a flipchart containing the six principles related to witnessing to a person, page 94.
- Prepare flipchart listing five major factors in a systematic program of visitation, page 98.
- Plan to ask each class member to choose one other person in his small group and relate his own salvation experience in Christ. Take not more than ten minutes. *It could well be that this will be the most important teaching procedure you will use.*
- Discuss Sunday School outreach plans. A definite recommendation should be made to the church concerning these plans.

Chapter 9

- Prepare a strip chart to bring out three conditions which must be changed in our churches. They are:
    1. Unregenerate lives
    2. Uncommitted and undisciplined lives
    3. Lives that show little love

  Treat each point positively and discuss ways to bring about change. Reveal each point as you discuss it by removing the strip of paper over it.
- Open your Bible and read the various Scripture verses which show the different kinds of "calls" to which the dedicated Christian must be committed. They are:
    1. The basic call of discipleship (Matt. 16:24–25)
    2. The call to holy living (Rom. 12:1–2)
    3. The call to the servant's role (Matt. 20:26–28.)

  Discuss as desired.

Chapter Outlines

II. Man's Primary Need

III. Three Foundational Tasks

    1. Outreach
    2. Bible Teaching
    3. Christian Living
    4. Outreach, Bible Teaching, Performance

IV. Related Church Actions Toward Mature Discipleship

    1. Giving Orientation to New Church Members
    2. Teaching Other Content Areas
    3. Training for Christian Performance
    4. Leadership Training—Potential and Specialized

V. Needs and Goals Summarized

Chapter 3

Understanding and Applying the Principles of Enlargement

I. Principles of Enlargement Stated

    1. The Principle of Leadership
    2. The Principle of Delegation
    3. The Principle of Grouping
    4. The Principle of Involvement of Learners
    5. The Principle of Visitation
    6. The Principle of Organization
    7. The Principle of Space and Facilities
    8. The Principle of Relationship

II. Principles of Enlargement Applied

    1. Know Your Possibilities
    2. Enlarge the Organization
    3. Provide the Needed Space
    4. Enlist and Train the Workers
    5. Go After the People

Chapter 4

Identifying the Possibilities for Enlargement

I. Areas for Enlargement

    1. Possibilities for Enlargement Within the Church

2. Possibilities for Enlargement Beyond the Church

II. PURPOSES OF A PROSPECT SEARCH

1. To Discover Unsaved People and Inactive Church Members
2. To Locate Places for Missions or New Sunday Schools
3. To Accept Opportunities for Witnessing

III. TYPES OF PROSPECT SEARCH

1. Inside Census
2. Church Community Religious Census

IV. PLANNING THE PROSPECT SEARCH

1. Determine the Type Search to Be Conducted
2. Set Aside Calendar Time
3. Order Necessary Supplies
4. Enlist Necessary Workers
5. Prepare Census Assignments
6. Instruct the Workers

V. CONDUCTING THE PROSPECT SEARCH

1. Check Out Assignments
2. Insist That Workers Follow Instructions
3. Check In the Assignments

VI. PROCESSING THE RESULTS OF THE SEARCH

1. Coding the Cards
2. Preparing Enrolment Prospect Visitation Forms
3. Refiling the Cards

VII. USING THE INFORMATION RECEIVED

Chapter 5

Organizing for Enlargement

I. RESPONSIBILITY FOR ORGANIZATION

1. The Responsibility of the Church Staff
2. The Responsibility of Other Church Officers
3. The Responsibility of the Church

II. EXTENT OF ORGANIZATION

1. Study the Present Organization
2. Study the Possibilities of Enlargement
3. Determine the Need for New Units, Now and in the Future

4. Acknowledge Any Limitations the Church May Face
5. Be Guided by the Principles Which Determine Growth
6. In Faith, Agree on the New Units to Be Added

Chapter 6

Providing Space and Equipment for Enlargement

I. Recognizing the Importance of Space and Equipment

II. Conducting a Critical Church Space Survey

1. Surveying Available Space
2. Adjusting the Use of Space
3. Adapting the Use of Space

III. Planning for New Space

1. A Survey and Planning Committee
2. A Church Building Committee
3. Consultation

IV. Furnishings and Equipment Needs

1. Furnishings Should Be Graded
2. Furnishings Should Be Ordered in Time
3. Establish Specifications

V. Counting the Cost

1. The Building Budget
2. The Building Fund
3. Borrowed Funds

Chapter 7

Enlisting and Training Workers for Enlargement

I. Determine Basic Qualifications for Workers

II. Enlist Sunday School Workers

1. Pinpoint the Vacancies
2. Prepare to Discover Potential Workers
3. Gather Materials
4. Conduct the Meeting
5. Plan the Contacts
6. Make the Contact

III. Plan to Train Sunday School Workers

    1. The Leaders Responsible for Sunday School Training
    2. Types of Training

Chapter 8

Going After People—the Purpose of Enlargement

I. Developing Christian Concern

    1. The Pastor and the Deacons
    2. The Church Council
    3. The Sunday School Officers and Teachers
    4. The Sunday School Members

II. Developing Christian Witnesses

    1. The Life of the Witness
    2. The Skill of the Witness
    3. A Plan for Development

III. Organizing and Conducting a Program of Enlistment

    1. Using a Prospect File
    2. Visitation to Reach
    3. A Plan for Prospect Visitation
    4. Visitation That Evidences Concern
    5. Meaningful Involvement to Hold

Chapter 9

Becoming a Church That Can Go

I. Trends Which Must Be Faced

II. Conditions Which Must Be Changed

    1. Unregenerate Lives
    2. Uncommitted and Undisciplined Lives
    3. Lives That Show Little Love

III. Commitments Which Must Be Made

    1. The Basic Call of Discipleship
    2. The Call to Holy Living
    3. The Call to the Servant's Role

IV. COMMANDS WHICH MUST BE OBEYED

1. To Witness
2. To Make Disciples
3. To Equip the Disciples
4. To Represent Christ in Life and Work

The Church Study Course

The Church Study Course consists of a variety of short-term credit courses for adults and youth and noncredit foundational units for children and preschoolers. The materials are for use in addition to the study and training curriculums made available to the churches on an ongoing basis.

Study courses and foundational units are organized into a system that is promoted by the Sunday School Board, 127 Ninth Avenue, North, Nashville, Tennessee 37234; by the Woman's Missionary Union, 600 North Twentieth Street, Birmingham, Alabama 35203; by the Brotherhood Commission, 1548 Poplar Avenue, Memphis, Tennessee 38104; and by the respective departments of the state conventions affiliated with the Southern Baptist Convention.

Study Course materials are flexible enough to be adapted to the needs of any Baptist church. The resources are published in several different formats—textbooks of various sizes, workbooks, and kits. Each item contains a brief explanation of the Church Study Course and information on requesting credit. Additional information and interpretation are available from the participating agencies.

Types of Study and Credit

Adults and youth can earn study course credit through individual or group study. Youth may take adult courses for credit, but adults can receive credit for youth courses only by teaching them to youth. Teachers of courses or of foundational units are eligible to receive credit.

1. *Class Experience.*—Group involvement with course material for the designated number of hours for the particular course. A person who is absent from one or more sessions must complete the "Personal Learning Activities" or other requirements for the material missed.
2. *Individual Study.*—This includes reading course material and completing the specified requirements for the course.
3. *Lesson Course Study.*—Parallel use of designated study course material during the study of selected units in Church Program Organization periodical curriculum units. Guidance for this means of credit appears in the selected periodical.
4. *Institutional Study.*—Parallel use of designated study course material during regular courses at educational institutions, including Seminary Extension Department courses. Guidance for this means of credit is provided by the teacher.

Credit is awarded for the successful completion of a course of study. This credit is granted by the Church Study Course Awards Office, 127 Ninth Avenue, North, Nashville, Tennessee 37234, for the participating agencies Form 151 (available free) is recommended for use in requesting credit.

When credit is issued to a person on request, the Awards Office sends two copies of a notice of credit earned to the church. The original copy of the credit slip should be filed by the study course clerk in the participant's record of training folder. The duplicate should be given to the person who earned the credit. Accumulated credits are applied toward leadership or member development diplomas, which are measures of learning, growth, development, and training.

Detailed information about the Church Study Course system of credits, diplomas, and record keeping is available from the participating agencies. Study course materials, supple-

mentary teaching or learning aids and forms for record keeping may be ordered from Baptist Book Stores.

The Church Study Course Curriculum

Credit is granted on those courses listed in the current copy
of *Church Services and Materials Catalog* and *Baptist Book
Store Catalog.*

*When selecting courses or foundational units, the current
catalogs should be checked to determine what study course
materials are valid.*

How to Request Credit for This Course

This book is the text for a course in the Subject Area "Sunday
School Leadership." It is one of the six required books for
the Sunday School Leadership Diploma for General Officers.

This course is designated for 5 hours of group study. Credit is
awarded for satisfactory class experience with the study
material for the minimum number of hours. A person who is
absent for one or more sessions must complete the "Personal
Learning Activities" or other requirements for the material
missed.

Credit is also allowed for use of this material in individual
study, and in institutional study, if so designated by an
educational institution.

After the course is completed, the teacher, the study course
clerk, or any person designated by the church should complete Form 151 ("Church Study Course Credit Request, Re-

vised 1975") and send it to the Awards Office, 127 Ninth Avenue, North, Nashville, Tennessee 37234. Individuals also may request credit by writing the Awards Office. The form on the next page may be used.

Cut along this line

INSTRUCTIONS: If requested by the teacher, fill in this form and give it to him when the course is completed. If preferred, mail this request for course credit to

AWARDS OFFICE
THE SUNDAY SCHOOL BOARD, SBC
127 NINTH AVENUE, NORTH
NASHVILLE, TENNESSEE 37234

Indicate Type of Study (X)

☐ Class   ☐ Individual   ☐ Lesson Course   ☐ Educational Institution

CHURCH		
State Convention	Association	
Church Name		
Mailing Address		
City, State, Zip Code		

MAIL TO	
Mail to (If Different from Church Address)	
Street, Route, or P.O. Box	
City, State, Zip Code	

COURSE TITLE

A Guide to Sunday School Enlargement

LAST NAME	FIRST NAME AND MIDDLE INITIAL	MRS. (X)